DON'T PLAY IN THE STREET

...unless you know which way your stock is traveling

George Thompson

Dearborn™
Trade Publishing
A **Kaplan Professional** Company

Vice President and Publisher: Cynthia A. Zigmund
Acquisitions Editor: Mary B. Good
Senior Project Editor: Trey Thoelcke
Interior Design: Lucy Jenkins
Cover Design: Megan Monaghan
Typesetting: the dotted i

Published by Dearborn Trade Publishing, a Kaplan Professional Company

Printed in the United States of America

03   04   05   10 9 8 7 6 5 4 3 2 1

Library of Congress Cataloging-in-Publication Data

Thompson, George, 1965–
    Don't play in the street : unless you know which direction your stock is traveling / George Thompson
        p.   cm.
    Includes index.
    ISBN 0-7931-7926-2
    1. Stocks.   2. Investments.   I. Title.
HG4521.T467 2003
332.63'22—dc21

                                                              2003009722

DEDICATION

I dedicate this book to every individual investor who is willing to take advantage of the financial opportunities that the heritage of our great nation has provided. My greatest reward is to help the individual investor financially succeed in a marketplace where major institutions have historically dominated. Technology has made it possible for each of you to have the proper trading tools to succeed in any market environment.

Contents

After years of research and development a longtime dream of mine was fulfilled in 1999. I released the first version of the Wizetrade™ software. My deepest appreciation goes out to my good friend and partner, Marc A. Sparks, for helping me fulfil my personal dream of creating a system and an organization that allow individuals to create their own financial independence. Marc's vision and leadership have been the driving force behind the success of the Wizetrade™ program and the assembly of the finest group of individuals to create the company that exists today. Without Marc, this book would not exist, and neither would Wizetrade™, 4X Made Easy, or Options Made Easy. Here's to you Marc and that little ad you ran in the *Dallas Morning News* on December 5, 1999, that brought us together.

> ## Need Capital?
>
> Investment firm is seeking dynamic D/FW companies in need of capital. Owners must remain; companies must be at least one year old. (No restaurants.) Prefer e-commerce, high-tech business, and manufacturing, but will consider retail. Equity participating funds provides capital, management and marketing assistance where needed. Fax outline of capital needs, business summary and financials to Mr. Gwinn at 972-387-4830.

As a company, Wizetrade™ has come a very long way since we opened our doors. Now called GlobalTec Solutions, LLP, the company produces seven software products—Wizetrade™, Wizefinder™, Options Made Easy, Option Hunter, 4X Made Easy, LiquidTrader, Command Trade—and has developed training programs to help the average American participate in the financial opportunities provided by our capitalist system. I am very proud to be surrounded by the individuals that have made GlobalTec the company it is today.

Writing *Don't Play in the Street* was an interesting project and a bigger challenge than I initially expected. This book would have never been completed without the dedication of many friends and colleagues.

I am forever grateful to my partner, Marc Sparks, for his tremendous focus and dedication and to Marc's brother, Scott Sparks, for his insight into the art of fine writing. Their encouragement kept me motivated to stay with the project until the book came to fruition. Many times they would make me laugh and say just the right thing to create a spark that would lead to the completion of yet another chapter. Scott's uncanny ability to grasp this industry and add humor to this story made him a joy to work with.

Many other people have made major contributions and donated their precious time to creating this book as well. Claude deGuchi's outlook on the investment industry added valuable insight to the book and his editorial efforts are sincerely appreciated. A special thanks goes to Trish Coulman for keeping everyone involved, organized (just like she does with all of our projects), and focused on the task at hand. Thanks also to Megan Monaghan, the most talented graphic artist I know, who is one of the most dedicated people with whom I have had the opportunity to work. Megan and Marc Sparks work magic together. Finally, thanks to Susan Dufour who came to this organization with a background in the investment and software industries. Her dedication and knowledge of these two industries have provided powerful perspectives and insights for my book.

Thank you all and congratulations on a job very well done.

DON'T PLAY IN THE STREET
Unless You Know Which Direction
Your Stock Is Traveling

MISSION IMPOSSIBLE?

Heck no! *You* can make money on Wall Street by yourself and you can even *thrive* in these turbulent times. Forget about what brokers and analysts and the media tell you. After all, look where they led millions of Americans during the tough times   down a primrose path of misinformation if not outright lies. Throw out their old rules and start thinking like a professional trader. Open your mind and consider how you can take total control of your financial destiny.

My mission in writing this book is to level the playing field for individuals in the stock market against all those brokerage firms, market makers, analysts, and Wall Street crooks who let their self-interests and greed outweigh the ethical issues of helping their customers succeed.

I want you to beat the experts. *You* can. For me, satisfaction is watching the little guy beat the big guy, like David versus Goliath. It's not that I want to see the big guys fail, I just want the underdog to win. As an entrepreneur, I relate to the underdog because, by nature, entrepreneurs are underdogs—they blaze their own trails. It shouldn't surprise you that I have vivid and fond memories of enjoying *The Bad News Bears* as a young kid, cheering on society's rejects as they beat the best in the world.

My mission in this book is to prepare you to be an independent and empowered stock investor. I appreciate and understand that education is the key to accomplishing this mission. Once you are educated, you can confidently take charge of your finances. Therefore, you need to:

- Understand the institutions that are inherent players in the stock market and identify the pitfalls in dealing with those players due to their conflicts of interest
- Understand the ABCs of investing and trading
- Learn about the criteria and tools at your disposal to confidently choose your own investments

STOCKING UP

Let's be clear from the get go: This book is geared towards trading *stocks* for personal growth. Though I address the important topics of overall portfolio management as well as your risk tolerance and diversification strategies, this book is not intended to cover in depth any other kinds of investment, such as bonds, insurance, retirement accounts, and real estate. Only you can determine how much and what percentage of your money you can or want to invest in stocks.

Why stocks? Stocks have outperformed any other form of investment mechanism over the long term. This is because the U.S. market has enjoyed a continuous upward trend for well over a hundred years. Even through slumps and bear markets, you can thrive and make money—not just protect your current portfolio.

There are lucrative and sound investments out there during both bull markets and bear markets. Utilizing the right tools, stocks are by far the best investment in which to grow your money.

There is always an element of uncertainty with stocks no matter how wisely and safely you play it. That is why you need to devise a solid plan. To do this you need to follow some objectives so you know what you're striving for and can strategize a plan to reach your goals.

OBJECTIVES: TAKING STOCK

In general:

- Take control of your financial destiny
- Establish financial freedom and independence
- Build and control wealth

Regarding outside influences:

- Ignore most of the old rules—learn which ones you *don't* need to know!
- Disregard market gurus, full-service stockbrokers, and newsletters
- Cut out all the special interests of indifferent industrial entities
- Avoid the common mistakes and fallacies of investing

Regarding stocks in particular:

- Take the guesswork out of trading stocks
- Grasp what really drives stocks up and down
- Know what criteria to identify great opportunities
- Make trading choices simply, quickly, and reliably
- Pinpoint entry and exit signals (when to buy and sell) for your trading style
- Increase your profits and stop your losses
- Establish a method of trading that yields consistent positive results
- Manage your stock portfolio in minutes per day
- Make money in bull *and* bear markets

On a personal note:

- Identify your trading style and strategy
- Become proficient in your trading style
- Invest within your comfort level so you sleep well at night
- Devote only the time you need for your trading style
- Remove the emotions of fear and greed when trading by following your plan of action
- Get rid of shaky stocks in your portfolio now!
- Boost your personal trading confidence dramatically

Finally, invest only in "the best of the best"—not merely in stocks which are going up, but in those which have the most demand and meet all your good investing criteria.

Much of the material in this book seems simple (because it is), but I urge you to take your time to fully grasp it. As Abraham Lincoln once said, "Give me six hours to chop down a tree and I will spend the first four sharpening the axe." I suggest you keep a highlighter and pen or pencil handy as you go through the rest of the book. Underline, circle, highlight, write down your own notes, or do all of the above. This will keep you actively involved as you go through this guide and will give you quick reference later to the points of particular interest or concern to you.

The time you spend now preparing yourself to be a successful trader will pay off huge dividends and won't leave you with an axe to grind later.

Ready? I know you are. With basic education and some tools at your disposal to help you make sound investments in well-chosen stocks, I have full faith that you can succeed beyond whatever doubts you may have—and regardless of the whims of the stock market as a whole.

The goal is for you not only to be self-reliant but to assure your success.

1

WALL STREET SCANDALS

Same as It Ever Was

W h a t Y e a r W a s I t ?

Okay, let's play a little game. Guess the year of the following storyline and headline. Hint: They were both published in the *Wall Street Journal* in the same year within two months of each other.

Source: The Collection of the Museum of American Financial History

STORYLINE

"In a story like this, every story is a positive one. Any news is good news. It's pretty much taken for granted now that the market is going to go up."

HEADLINE

"Stocks Plunge 508 Amid Panicky Selling; Percentage Decline Is Far Steeper than in 1929"

The answer can be found later in this chapter.

Let's open with a little story that may sound all too familiar.

A speculator creates a new company, financed with huge sums of money from banks and rich friends. This company quickly evolves into a financial empire and the the original speculator becomes fabulously wealthy. Suspecting insider chicanery, the government orders the company's books be audited. Outrageous amounts of money are found missing. The government sues the company's president and carts him off to jail.

In the wake of the scandal, the company's empire collapses, bankrupting many creditors, bankers, and brokers and causing a financial panic on Wall Street. The Secretary of the Treasury meets with prominent brokers to set rules to regulate trading. He proclaims that "there should be a separation between honest men and knaves . . . between respectable stockbrokers . . . and mere unprincipled gamblers."

This story is true. At the time, it was an outrage and a scandal, and it introduced a time-honored American tradition.

It is the story of what's been dubbed Wall Street's first scandal—in 1792. The "knave" was William Duer who used his insider knowledge (he was once Assistant Secretary of the U.S. Treasury) to speculate in and manipulate bank stocks. The amount found missing was $238,000—a heap of cash in 1792. And the Secretary of the Treasury who's quoted here was none other than Alexander Hamilton. You may have noticed his picture on the ten-dollar bill.

FLASH FORWARD TO THE YEAR 2002

Today, most economic historians and analysts aren't surprised by the revelations of all the shenanigans that have surfaced since Enron filed for bankruptcy in December 2001. Hindsight helps, because only a couple of them predicted our present predicament just a few years ago in the late 1990s.

Much of America's grand and glorious financial history has been marked by cycles of Wall Street scandals. Typically, the cycle goes like this:

- There's a period of unparalleled prosperity like the one we enjoyed through the late 1990s. Everyone's making money so everyone's happy. Don't fix it if it ain't broke.
- The bubble finally bursts and countless hordes lose their shirts.
- Hard questions are asked that should have been asked throughout the prosperous period.

- Probes lead to unpleasant answers, revelations of books being cooked, forced resignations, lawsuits, and criminal investigations.
- The Securities and Exchange Commission, prosecutors, Congress, and the president all condemn the scoundrels and float ideas for new regulations to prevent future scandals.
- Insulted but contrite, Wall Street promises to clean up its act and vows it can self-regulate with no more new laws or restrictions.
- Wall Street returns to business as usual.

A line from a Peggy Lee song comes to mind: "If that's all there is, my friend, then let's keep dancing."

The most recent corporate audacity and misbehavior are mind-blowing. The trillions of dollars that went down the tubes is breathtaking and there's plenty of blame to spread around.

A *Washington Post* article on June 28, 2002, quotes the dean of Yale University's School of Management, Jeffrey E. Garten.

> I think it's fair to say that there was nobody in the business community who is not implicated in this in some way. Not the executives who were under the excruciating pressure of having to meet quarterly earnings targets, no matter what. Not the lawyers and the accountants and bankers who were forced to compete furiously to get and keep clients. Not the regulators who became so intimidated by all the exuberance in the air. Certainly not the underwriters or the analysts or the credit-rating agencies or you in the press. . . . Even those of us at business schools are implicated. It's not like the educational establishment sounded any warning. We were cheerleaders, too.

But don't kid yourself that this is something new. Sure, there's been a meltdown of dot-com and telecom companies that didn't exist in days of yore. But the scandals and allegations of law-breaking and insider trading at companies like Enron, WorldCom, Merrill Lynch, and Tyco only earns them a spot in the rogue's gallery that we might dub the Wall Street Hall of Shame. They're far from being the original inductees.

To quote Robert Reich, former labor secretary:

> Really, there is no limit to the cons and swindles that have been seen over the years. The human mind is capable of inventing very innovative products and services—and also extraordinarily innovative swindles.

The corporate chicanery uncovered in recent scandals has been an integral part of every burst bubble since the 17th century Dutch tulip mania. (More about bubbles later.)

Some great names in American history made their fortunes through shameless swindling—Vanderbilt, Morgan, Rockefeller, and Kennedy to name a few. Do you only relate these names with their philanthropy? Perhaps their consciences finally got the better of them when mortality stared them down.

Financial crooks tend to be respectable folks who demonstrate their patriotism by giving vast sums of money to America's politicians, asking nothing in return except maybe a tweak in the tax code, in the smallest print possible, benefiting their industry.

In the election year of 2002, Republicans and Democrats alike were jockeying for sound bites to pronounce that their side had taken and will continue to take the high road. Each side was biting at the bit to blame the other side for letting this mess unfold. Yet candidates from both parties had received campaign contributions from Enron, WorldCom, and Arthur Andersen. These companies contributed millions of dollars to our lawmakers.

Okay, let's take a moment to enjoy another true story. This one is from the 1800s. *Washington Post* staff writer Peter Carlson's February 10, 2002, article contributed the details of these scams of yore.

CIVIL WAR AND THE LIVING IS EASY

Many of the Civil War–era's robber barons dodged the draft by paying someone $300 to fight in their place. We're talking J.P. Morgan, John D. Rockefeller, Andrew Carnegie, and Jay Gould. Their small investments gave them the opportunity to avoid getting shot, thereby leaving them free to get rich during the war.

During the war, Morgan arranged a deal to buy 5,000 rifles from a Union Army arsenal in New York for $3.50 apiece. He turned around and sold the rifles to the Union Army in Virginia for $22 each. A judge ruled the deal was legal, even though the rifles were defective causing soldiers to shoot their thumbs off.

Some on Wall Street speculated in gold. The gold rose in price, rising against the dollar, with each defeat of the Union Army. Getting wind of this, President Lincoln made it clear that he hoped that every gold speculator "had his devilish head shot off."

After the war, the railroad business provided these entrepreneurs with easily their biggest payoff. According to Mr. Carlson's account of this episode:

> In the 1860s, the federal government subsidized the building of a transcontinental railroad by granting millions of acres of free land to two railroad companies, the Union Pacific and the Southern Pacific. Eager to line their pockets at the expense of their stockholders, Union Pacific management formed a dummy construction company with an impressive-sounding French name, Credit Mobilier, and hired Rep. Oakes Ames as president. Credit Mobilier charged Union Pacific about $100 million to build the railroad—nearly twice what the job actually cost. The rest of the money went to Credit Mobilier's stockholders, a group that included many of Ames's congressional cronies and Vice President Schuyler Colfax, who had been bribed with cheap stock to look the other way.

Congressional hearings were held and there were angry editorials and a federal lawsuit. Ultimately, the Credit Mobilier scammers went their merry way, far richer for their modest efforts. Viva America! And Credit Mobilier!

One more side note from this era: President Ulysses S. Grant was scammed by a Wall Street crook and lost his fortune.

BUBBLE, BUBBLE, BOIL AND TROUBLE

A speculative bubble is a period when stock prices rise to unsustainable levels, driven primarily by investor optimism when they speculate—that is, when they guess or rely on gut instinct or emotions—that one or more stocks or industries will skyrocket. Speculators engage in risky business transactions on the chance of making quick and vast profits. Optimism is contagious so the bubble grows as others join the frenzy. Who wants to miss out on what seems to be a sure bet?

But when the bubble bursts—the speculators' "crik" comes up empty where gold nuggets were expected—investors jump ship and sell their stocks that are dramatically losing value every moment. Stocks sometimes lose over half their value in no time flat, and those stocks hardest hit may remain depressed for years. Some never recover. The companies either go out of business or they're absorbed by stronger companies. The market becomes survival of the fittest.

The late 1990s was an example of a speculative bubble. (Ain't hindsight great?) During this period, the Nasdaq Composite Index, representing many of technology's "red hot" dot-com and telecom stocks, rose sharply, peaking at 5,048 in March 2000. Eighteen months later, the Nasdaq fell to 1,423. The dot-com and telecom stocks that flooded the market accounted for most of the rapid growth and even more rapid depreciation of the Nasdaq.

Today, many of those companies are floundering or no longer exist. The speculators in those stocks lost trillions of dollars, devastating many retirement funds and leaving hundreds of thousands of employees scrambling for new jobs. Was there any forewarning? Did history provide any lessons that we should have heeded? After all, we know that history has a habit of repeating itself.

Perhaps present-day speculators should have taken a gander at past bubbles that burst, namely:

- The late 1920s just before the 1929 crash
- The period between 1970 and 1972
- The period between 1982 and 1987

In each case, you can recognize the cycle of scandals and scams repeating itself.

Let's take a closer look at the 1929 crash as it relates to our current bubble-and-burst scenario.

1929: THE NIGHTMARE ON WALL STREET

In the early 1920s, the climate for great business was super. The president proclaimed "the business of America is business." Between 1926 and September of 1929, U.S. stocks soared to euphoric heights. The market was pumped up by corporate profits, the government's probusiness policies, and deals allowing stock to be purchased for only 10 percent down.

Near the peak, some prominent economists and bankers debated about whether the market would sustain a boom or succumb to a bust. Those who predicted a crash were criticized and scorned into silence as party poopers. The rabid speculators who were caught up in stock mania favored the "experts" who were predicting that the market reached a plateau of new heights that would sustain itself forever more. The feeling was the market would never go lower.

In September 1929, the limits of demand and available capital for investing were sorely tested. The market drifted slightly lower, and then selling built into a deluge. Panic ensued. During two October days, more than $9 billion of the market value of American business was erased, leaving prices 25 percent lower. That was the infamous crash of the stock market.

Far more devastating to the country and the entire world was the depression that followed. Stock prices bottomed 90 percent below their 1929 highs in the aftermath of what is probably the most far-reaching and widely felt speculative bubble in economic history.

Let's look at the numbers.

Year	Date	News
1929	September 3	Dow Jones peaks at 381
	October 28	Dow Jones, 260
	October 29	Dow Jones, 230
1930	April 17	Dow Jones, 294 (a rise, what's the deal?)
1932	July 8	Dow Jones falls to 41! (a 90 percent decline from its peak on September 3, 1929)

After the stock market crashed in 1929, Congress investigated and uncovered countless instances of skullduggery, chicanery, and unadulterated fraud.

In one notable example, Ivar Krueger, a Swedish entrepreneur known as the "match king," acquired monopolies to control two-thirds of the world's kitchen match industry. He controlled his companies through an illegal pyramid-based holding company. When the pyramid collapsed during the Great Depression, Krueger shot himself.

In 1934, five years *after* the crash, the federal government finally created the Securities and Exchange Commission to regulate and police the stock market, which had always enjoyed the privilege of regulating itself. Incensed, Richard Whitney, president of the New York Stock Exchange, told Congress that the stock exchange didn't need an overseer and that they could police themselves without bureaucratic interference, thank you very much.

In 1937, Whitney was caught stealing $150,200 worth of bonds belonging to the New York Yacht Club and $667,000 from the Stock Exchange Gratuity Fund which had been set up to aid the widows and orphans of brokers. He demanded that the stock exchange cover up his crimes because, in his words, to millions of people "I *mean* the stock market." Instead, he was sentenced to five to ten years in Sing Sing.

THEN AND NOW

Far more than any other precedent, present-day historians, economists, and columnists are comparing the bubble and burst we're experiencing today to that of 1929 and the period that followed. Few predict that we're now facing a depression like that of 70 years ago, but any comparison of our present predicament to the "worst of times" is sobering, considering its consequences in the past.

The 1920s stock market investor knew little about the stocks he bought or sold. Investors moved in herds in and out of stocks based on news events, hot tips, or the actions of the ticker tape. Even as their stocks plummeted, they hated to sell them because everyone told them not to.

Today, we no longer have the cumbersome ticker tape, but our increased access to moment-by-moment stock market fluctuations becomes more dangerous because today's investor is generally not any more savvy to what really moves the market and is prone to making even quicker knee-jerk decisions on his holdings. Investments still are based too much on emotions—namely greed and fear. And misplaced loyalty still leads investors to hold onto a losing proposition. We wouldn't want to disappoint our broker, would we?

Also, the technology of the 1920s runs strikingly parallel to the tech boom of the 1990s. For example, at its peak, the auto industry was comprised of close to 2,000 carmakers. It was an exciting and heady days for investors. Today the auto industry is dominated by only a handful of companies, only two of which are wholly American.

In the 1990s, it seemed, there were hundreds of Internet companies on the stock exchange and investors poured huge sums of money into companies that had yet to earn a penny, had no business plans other than to do "something" on the Internet, and were run by cocky twenty-somethings. Again, history was repeating itself. Like the auto industry, the vast majority of Internet companies from the late 1990s have either tanked and died or consolidated with the few survivors. That's the way it works. Always has, always will.

In both scenarios, devoted investors who worshipped at the temple of the tech market went from rags to riches to rags again, and somehow we're shocked? During both decades, unscrupulous corporations, accountants, and brokers were more than willing to string us along and prey on our gullibility because they made money every time a stock was sold. They smugly used insider information (and, more recently, computer projections programmed at a level that no human brain can digest) to pull the plug on their own investments when the bubble began to burst. And who's left to hold the empty bag? Not them. I guess that leaves us.

None of what went on in the 1920s or the 1990s would have been possible without the cooperation of the investing public. Human emotion and public euphoria led to speculation and set the stage for both bubbles—and busts.

What *is* different today is that stock ownership is no longer the sole domain of the rich, the daredevils, and the fools. The middle class became fully vested, and therefore vulnerable, even if their only involvement was through their 401(k)s at work. Now, when corporations, accountants, and the brokers have conflicts of interests that favor the "big boys" instead of the "little" investors, we are all prone to suffer the consequences.

Are you up for one more episode? This one's from the 1980s just so we don't make the mistake of only relegating scandals to the distant past.

GREED IS GOOD

Taxpayers lost hundreds of billions of dollars in depositor bailouts during the savings-and-loan crisis of the 1980s. Though fraud played a role, the problem resulted mainly from incredible mismanagement.

But what do we remember most leading up to the crash in 1987? Okay, I'll personalize it—what do I remember most? On "Black Monday" in October 1987, I had capitalized a brokerage firm (but was not a broker myself, my two brothers were licensed brokers in my company). I vividly remember that brokers all across America took their phones off the hook so that they could sell their own positions first before helping their bigwig clients bail out. The individual investors got a busy signal until after the institutional investors were taken care of. I couldn't get through to my *own* broker during that crash! (To ensure that this doesn't happen again, the Small Order Executive System (SOES) was created to execute agency orders in Nasdaq stocks (1,000 shares or less) to bypass the bias of brokers toward their biggest customers.)

What led up to this stock market loss of 508 points—20 percent—in a single day, exceeding the percentage decline of the crash of 1929? (If you're paying attention, I just answered the trivia question at the beginning of this chapter.) The loss largely was based on a huge decline in investor confidence due to scandals. Surprise.

You may remember the "greed is good" speech delivered by Michael Douglas in the 1987 movie *Wall Street*. He played a slick but chilling character named Gordon Gekko. But did you know that his speech was based almost word for word on a speech given by Ivan Boesky to some business students in 1985? Boesky told the students, "Greed is all right, by the way—I want you to know that. I think greed is healthy. You can be greedy and still feel good about yourself."

Boesky didn't just talk the talk, he walked the walk. After making hundreds of millions of dollars on stocks and bonds, he wanted more. Much more. He admitted fantasizing about climbing atop a huge pile of silver dollars because it would be an "aphrodisiac experience." Boesky then paid millions of dollars to an investment banker named Dennis Levine with Drexel Burnham Lambert for insider information on corporate takeovers. Boesky made millions more on insider trading.

The SEC caught Levine who ratted on Boesky. Boesky then ratted on many other wheeler-dealers, including Michael Milken, Drexel's legendary "junk bond king." Boesky acquired incriminating evidence on Milken by luring him into a hotel room and recording their conversation about their elaborate insider trading network.

Boesky served 18 months in prison and paid a $100 million fine. Milken served three years and paid $200 million. Drexel Burnham Lambert went bankrupt. A fellow named Rudolph Giuliani made his mark prosecuting all of these guys.

Unlike its delayed reaction after the 1929 crash, when it took the government five years to intervene in a significant way by creating the SEC, the government stepped in immediately after the 1987 crash. The Federal Reserve guaranteed the credit of market makers the day after the crash and a recession was averted. But it gave investors the faulty impression that the government's intervention could solve every pesky tumble off the cliff.

THE WRITING WAS ON THE WALL

Okay, let's look at a timeline of the most recent movement of the market from 1998 to mid-2002, including the intrusion of scandals as the bubble burst. With your newly heightened insight into the cycle of scandals, I'll refrain from interpreting the events for you and present just the facts, ma'am. (See Figure 1.1.)

FIGURE 1.1 *The Rise and Fall of the Stock Market from 1998 to Mid-2002*

Year	Date	News
1998	April 6	Dow Jones closes above 9,000 for first time
1999	March 29	Dow closes above 10,000 for first time
2000	January 14	Dow hits record high of 11,722.98
	March 20	Nasdaq hits record high of 5,048.62
	March 16	Dow rises 499.19 points, biggest point gain on record
The tide starts to turn:		
2000	December 31	Dow and Nasdaq both record **a losing year for the first time since 1990**
2001	January 3	Nasdaq jumps a record 14.17% after Fed makes a surprise rate cut
	Early March	Nasdaq's gain from two months earlier is gone
	September 17	Market opens following terrorist attacks; Dow records biggest point drop in history, falling 684.41
	December 2	Enron files for bankruptcy
	December 31	Markets **fall for a second straight year, first time since 1974**
2002	January 2	Kmart files for bankruptcy
	January 24	Arthur Andersen accounting firm admits destroying Enron documents
	March 13	SEC launches WorldCom probe
	April 25	SEC launches formal investigation of Wall Street analysts' conflict of interests
	May 7	SEC's Pitt denies conflict of interest in Xerox probe
	May 21	Merrill Lynch settles conflict of interest case related to analysts, prosecuted by NY Attorney General Spitzer. Fine: $100 million.
	June 3	Tyco CEO quits; Knight Trading discrepancies made public
	June 15	Arthur Andersen found guilty of obstructing justice when it shredded Enron documents
	June 25	WorldCom says it overstated cash flow by $3.8 billion; SEC calls it an accounting misstep of "unprecedented magnitude"
	June 30	Markets continue **fall at end of 2nd quarter**, 2002, **possibly signaling a fall for a third straight year, the first time since 1941**

AND THE POINT IS . . .

Let history be your guide. Expect lies, exaggerations, or, far more prevalent, silence from companies' top executives who, when questioned about specifics of their business practices, proclaim "we don't talk about that." You know what? You can take your money elsewhere. If they ask why, you can reply "I don't talk about that."

When scandals hit, don't let it throw you. It's happened before and will happen again.

Remember, the stock market exists to bring together those with a surplus of money (investors) and those who need money to finance enterprise (companies). If you have any hint that the company that needs investment money is not to be trusted, don't give it your money. And never give money to a company that has a "cool concept" but has yet to earn a dollar. In either case, say adios and don't look back.

A healthy dose of cynicism will serve you well. Trust it. Caveat emptor. Buyer beware.

Don't expect to get rich overnight. But know that there are lucrative and sound investments out there—during both bull markets and bear markets.

We—meaning you and I—can do far better if we know the score. Trust yourself. I'll do my damnedest to give you the knowledge and tools you need to do that. That's what this book is all about.

QUOTE UNQUOTE

I find these two quotes very interesting:

1. "Those who cannot remember the past are condemned to repeat it." (George Santayana)
2. "If past history was all there was to the game, the richest people would be librarians." (Warren Buffett, legendary investor)

I'd rather be rich than a librarian.

Now let's shine a light behind the curtain to expose the major players on Wall Street. As you'll see, the conflicts of interest inherent in every important institution that drives Wall Street stack the deck in their favor and purposefully leave you in the dark. Will any of these conflicts be resolved in the uproar over the current scandals and crises of confidence? I'm following the story just like you.

But it's very important for you to understand how Wall Street works, even if it isn't pretty. You'll quickly recognize that most of their BS is irrelevant to you as a successful investor if you don't buy into their games. With that said, let me introduce the cast of characters.

W h a t   Y e a r   W a s   I t ?

Here's the answer to the trivia question at the top of this chapter: The year was 1987.

STORYLINE

"In a story like this, every story is a positive one. Any news is good news. It's pretty much taken for granted now that the market is going to go up."
Wall Street Journal, August 26, 1987, the day after the 1987 market peak.

HEADLINE

"Stocks Plunge 508 Amid Panicky Selling; Percentage Decline Is Far Steeper than in 1929"
Wall Street Journal, October 20, 1987, the day after the crash—just eight weeks after the peak.

LIARS AND TRICKSTERS AND BROKERS, OH MY!

Ninety-nine percent of brokerage analysts are giving the remaining 1 percent a bad reputation.

JON D. MARKMAN, managing editor, MSN MoneyCentral, May 31, 2002

In preparing this book, I came across a study that astounded even me.

For the year 2000 (when the bubble burst on Wall Street), researchers at the University of California and Stanford reviewed almost 40,000 stock recommendations from 213 brokerages. The brokerages' most highly rated stocks (those with "buy" or "strong buy" recommendations) had a negative 31 percent return compared to the rest of the stock market. The stocks rated as "sells" by these same brokerage firms—that is, the lowest rated stocks—outperformed the stock market by a positive 49 percent.

Let's be clear: Compared to the rest of the stock market in 2000, the highest recommendations from brokerages plunged 31 percent and sell recommendations gained by 49 percent. The dogs outperformed the winners by 80 percent! You would have made a bundle investing in the opposite of Wall Street's analysts recommendations.

Tulipomania

The tulip was a non-Western flower (originally from Turkey) that came into a boom market in the early 17th Century when an Austrian botanist who cultivated them in Western Europe fled to Holland to escape religious persecution. The flowers thrived in the Dutch climate and, soon, they became the rage among all classes of people. Those with money bought the flowers and planted them in lavish gardens to signify their wealth and power. The common man admired the flowers from afar. The national demand for this springtime flower soon became frenzied, and Tulipomania was born.

One of the largest factors contributing to the craze was the shift from the sale of tulips by the bulb to their sale by weight. The rarer the flower, the more it cost. The demand soon outgrew the supply, and people began trading on what was basically a nonexistent commodity—that is, the flower was being traded but what the buyer got was a bulb that, in essence, had the potential to become a flower. Soon, the speculative nature of the trade began to draw criticism and even ridicule, and the term *wind trade* was devised to show the whimsical and empty nature of the trades (determining prices out of thin air). Regardless, the trade was driven by the greed of the individuals participating in it, and even the government could do little to stop the momentum of the beast that was Tulipomania.

At a certain point, the demand (that is, the price) of the bulbs became so ridiculous that the market could no longer sustain it. It's said that Tulipomania ended in 1637 when a group of sellers came to the market and no one could afford to buy from them anymore. News spread and people started ditching their investment in droves, driving down the price faster than the Titanic sank. Most of those who stayed in the market to the bitter end were left with nothing except huge debts that they couldn't pay off.

What can we learn from this story? Greed spawns money-making schemes. Hindsight is 20/20. And always find a fool to pay a higher price or get the hell out of the market before you are left with nothing.

BUY, HOLD, SELL

The three basic recommendations given by brokers are to buy a stock, hold a stock, and sell a stock. You'd expect them to be equally weighted, especially in a bear market, but think again. Thomson Financial/First Call, a global research network, as reported in *Fortune* magazine's February 5, 2001, issue, kept a tally of the buy and strong buy recommendations as well as the sell recommendations of the ten largest investment banks. Here are the results.

Merrill Lynch	940 buys / 7 sells
Salomon Smith Barney	865 buys / 4 sells
Credit Suisse First Boston	791 buys / 9 sells
Goldman Sachs	780 buys / 4 sells
UBS Walburg	696 buys / 8 sells
Morgan Stanley Dean Witter	670 buys / 0 sells
Lehman Brothers	705 buys / 8 sells
Bank of America Securities	557 buys / 6 sells
Deutsche Banc Alex. Brown	513 buys / 9 sells
Bear Stearns	525 buys / 2 sells
Total:	**7,033 buys / 57 sells**

These are incredibly influential firms who issued buy or strong buy recommendations over 99 percent of the time compared to recommendations to sell (less than 1 percent). Is it any wonder that the "buy" mentality created by these firms, especially when steered to invest in their institutional clients' stocks, performed so poorly?

Seasoned investors know that Wall Street analysts refrain from issuing sell recommendations until the stock has neared bottom. Why? Because they face tremendous conflicts of interest within their firms to placate the most profitable end of their business—their institutional clients. The brokerages make a very small percentage of their money in commissions from individual investors' compared to the massive investment banking and consulting fees they can charge companies, especially those with an initial public offering (IPO). And the brokerages themselves have invested millions of dollars in loans to prop up these companies; why undercut the money flow by issuing a less than stellar rating?

Of course, these same brokerages and their preferred clients, possessing the inside knowledge of a company's poor performance, will sell their stock in droves while you and I are encouraged to keep buying, thus retaining the stock's value while they bail out. These firms count on us to be the lemmings who unwittingly fall off the cliff while they set sail to prosperity in their yachts.

In my estimation, this is a massive breach of trust between these firms and the general investing public.

WHEN THE TIDE TURNED

Prior to May 1975, price competition for commissions on investment transactions were illegal. Commission prices were fixed. Imagine, competition was not allowed on Wall Street, the ultimate symbol of capitalism.

The fat cats in this big gentlemen's club raked in big bucks every time someone invested in the market. You probably would have paid your stockbroker hundreds of dollars in commissions to invest $10,000 in stocks. But then, analysts also had the incentive to make profitable stock picks in order to retain their clients and keep them from going down the street and paying the same price for better advice.

On May 1, 1975 (known as "May Day" in the industry), the SEC deregulated set prices for commissions and allowed negotiation. May Day spelled the end of Wall Street's guaranteed good times; brokerage houses predicted doom and gloom at the time. When a small handful of brokers like Charles Schwab offered discount prices for transactions, breaking up the old gentlemen's club, the old-school Wall Street denizens had to scramble to find other ways to make money.

The deregulation of pricey commissions opened the market beyond the realm of the wealthy, the gamblers, and the fools. The middle class could now afford to play the game. But . . . be careful what you wish for.

Analysts and brokers turned to investment banking to rake in new revenue. The big bucks now came from juicy underwriting deals to provide initial public offerings of stock for new companies. The hunger for trading commissions dwindled until it was only a small piece of the pie.

During this transition, the analysts' incentive shifted dramatically from providing profitable stock tips for the powerful good old boys to supporting their firm's dealmakers in marketing the stock of their deep-pocketed clients. Analysts' objectivity gave way to promoting a product. An analyst's objectivity is obviously hampered if his firm's client pays outlandish fees to offer suspicious stock to the public. What to do? If he rocks the boat by giving his honest opinion of the stock's value, he would most likely lose his job.

Here's something to remember: Investors should always view a research report from a brokerage house as a sales product. A savvy investor can still glean some nuggets of truth in a good analyst's research report, just as you can study a car dealer's brochure to learn about the features of a new car. But for Pete's sake, ignore the recommendation to buy, hold, or sell. Like the car dealer, you know the broker wants you to buy what he's pitching, but maybe there's something else on his lot that's better for you. Or maybe nothing he has suits you. The choice to buy or pass is yours and yours alone.

I found a very good analogy provided in an interview on TheStreet.com with Benjamin Mark Cole, author of *The Pied Pipers of Wall Street: How Analysts Sell You Down the River*. He stated:

> I would say there are no impartial analysts, and no, there are no analysts who work for brokerages that I admire. Their job has become that of lawyers. They are not the judge in the courtroom, they are the lawyers in the courtroom. And the lawyers' job is to put forward the best case on behalf of their client. Whenever you hear an analyst speak, consider him a lawyer on behalf of his client. They may be telling the truth, but it may not be the whole truth.

Need an example? In 1999, Wall Street firms grossed $1 billion for bringing 214 Internet companies public. Investors paid over $16 billion for these IPOs. Today, the remaining companies may be worth $4 billion. Who paid for the investment bankers' profits? Investors who lost their shirts.

But this is America. Can't the government step in to resolve this conflict of interest mess by separating a brokerage firm's banking department from its investment department on which investors rely for "unbiased" advice? After all, the very foundation of a financial system must be built on the integrity of its information. The government has tried before, but it only resulted in "Chinese walls."

CHINESE WALLS

After the crash of 1929 that set the Great Depression in motion, the federal government needed to put in place some sense of accountability in investment banking practices that routinely crossed lines and created conflicts of interest. While the government could not physically separate brokerage firms from investment banks in large financial conglomerates, they passed the Glass-Steagall Act of 1933 that, in essence, placed barriers (or walls) between a company's banking and securities practices.

At a basic level, the relevant sections of Glass-Steagall state that a bank that is a member of the Federal Reserve cannot purchase securities for its own account. The rationale here is that if a bank is both buying stocks for itself *and* selling them to customers, it would have a conflicting interest in promoting and selling those stocks to the public in order to secure their own wealth, whether they were a good buy or not.

The result of this act is what is known as a Chinese wall (yes, the name was borrowed from the Great Wall of China). In the case of a large financial firm that offers both investment banking and securities services, the departments that deal with each area are supposed to be either physically or "ethically" separated from each other. This sounds like a great idea. The problem is that within the context of a company, the wall that exists between one department and another is flimsy at best.

If physicians freely discuss their patients with each other in a hospital setting, you can bet that bankers and analysts talk at the water cooler, too, but with much less discretion about ethical conduct.

While the *idea* of a Chinese wall is sound in theory, in reality, it doesn't work. The two parties on either side of the wall have too much to gain (such as millions, if not billions, of dollars) by commiserating with each other. The Pandora's box that's opened when the wall is traversed will *always* benefit the big clients, not the individual investors.

In 1999, under heavy lobbying pressure from investment banking firms, Congress actually struck down Glass-Steagall because investment bankers assured Congress that they could monitor themselves without it. In just three short years, the Chinese walls vanished and the departments on both sides joined together like Siamese twins.

That was the beginning of the end of the dot-com era. Investment bankers financed hundreds of fledgling companies that had "cool concepts" but had yet to earn a penny in revenue, and that was good enough for bullish optimism in the late 1990s. The bankers pressured their analysts—dragging them over the Chinese wall not with force but with the promise of making millions of dollars—to sell stocks to the gullible public during the bull market supporting these pie-in-the-sky dot-com companies. We would have been better off if they had thrown pies in our faces.

Fast-forward to 2002.

The government is once again cracking down on conflicts of interest at the major investment banking firms, whose analysts touted failing stocks during the last couple of years that cost the American public trillions of dollars in lost investments.

Gee, that didn't take long, now did it?

C h i n e s e W a l l

In a broader sense, *Chinese wall* is a term that also applies to the lines other than those drawn between investment banks and their analyst employees. It can refer to any relationship between entities where a line should be drawn—like between companies and independent accounting firms—but where that line can be easily crossed due to conflicts of interest. Unfortunately, a Chinese wall is only a concept, not an architectural barrier.

NOT SO FAST, MERRILL LYNCH

Only a few years ago, analysts lauded technology and telecommunications stocks that soared during the Internet bubble. After the crash that wiped out billions of dollars in paper wealth, regulators finally emerged from the shadows to investigate the relationship between investment banking and research on Wall Street that many had long said was riddled with conflicts of interest. (During the boom, there was little incentive to regulate or fix what wasn't broke until the consequences of neglect came to roost.)

In April 2002, state's attorney general Eliot Spitzer led a probe into the credibility of analysts' advice that triggered an uproar. He released e-mails that he obtained by subpoena, which showed that Merrill Lynch analysts in 2000 and 2001 often referred to an Internet stock as "a piece of crap" while issuing buy ratings for that same stock.

In the settlement, Merrill agreed to pay $100 million in fines. Individual investors got nothing. Zero. Instead, $48 million went to New York State and $52 million to other states.

To be fair to Merrill, they were not the only firm investigated by Eliot. The records of other major Wall Street firms also were subpoenaed, including those of Morgan Stanley Dean Witter & Co., Credit Suisse First Boston, the Salomon Smith Barney, Inc. unit of Citigroup, Inc., Lehman Brothers, Inc., Bear, Stearns & Co., UBS Warburg, and J.P. Morgan Chase & Co.

What changed after this settlement? Critics say very little. The settlement allows analysts to continue to work alongside investment bankers in some situations but is supposed to eliminate any investment banking incentives in setting analyst compensation. As part of the settlement, Merrill has agreed to base analysts' pay on stock-picking ability rather than investment banking work. However, as Jon D Markman pointed out on MSN MoneyCentral, "Brokerages have more elaborate systems for tracking how many phone calls the analysts make to clients pitching their research than they do for tracking whether the research makes sense."

Merrill and a couple other firms now under investigation have announced that they're adopting stricter standards of behavior, (if for no other reason than to regain some lost investors' confidence). But even as they announce plans for better behavior, brokerages still insist that their analysts always operated independently from their investment banking departments.

On BusinessWeek.com, Amey Stone cites a response from Barbara Roper, director of investor protection at the Consumer Federation of America: "I'm not convinced that bolstering investor confidence in Wall Street research really ought to be our goal. Perhaps bolstering a healthy skepticism about Wall Street research is a better goal, and Mr. Spitzer has certainly accomplished that."

ARE YOU READY FOR YOUR CLOSE-UP, MR. PITT? (HARVEY, NOT BRAD)

The Securities and Exchange Commission lists the potential conflicts of interests in surprisingly accessible language, covering bases I might have missed. For that I should thank Harvey Pitt, head of the SEC.

CONCLUSION

You can make far better sound investment choices—on your own—by eliminating inherent conflicts of interest in Wall Street's institutions. Second-guess your broker, not yourself. By pulling back the curtain to reveal the real Wizard of Oz, and realizing that he only has the power we give him, then you become the master of your own destiny.

The latter two-thirds of this book have been prepared to empower you to take control of your financial well being so you will not be at the mercy of outside powers beyond your control. With a little education and a few tools at your disposal to help take the guesswork out of sound investing in the stock market, I am confident that you can succeed.

MEDIA DARLINGS
But Not Your Darlin', Clementine

They say that a hero will save us. I'm not going to stand here and wait.

From the song "Hero," from the motion picture *Spider-Man*

As a whole, Americans have an umbilical cord connected to the television. More than any other nation in the world, TV in America is big business and entertainment. So it's no stretch of the imagination to realize that many Americans tune into their favorite daily investment news show before making investment decisions. Hey, if someone says it's so on TV, it must be true.

TV's financial shows typically feature a cast of characters who sit around, make predictions, and sound smooth and confident. The high-profile analysts on these shows are very similar to politicians. Like politicians, their task is to put on their best face and gain our trust. Because they're on TV, they become stars in our psyche. Just like in politics, the media darlings of the investment world are often willing to bend the truth or outright lie to you to convince you that they have your best interests at heart while selling you a bill of goods.

Star analysts for top rated firms (e.g., Henry Blodget of Merrill Lynch and Jack Grubman of Salomon Smith Barney) make upwards of $12 million in salary and bonuses per year, not because their opinions are worth being compensated at that level (then again, whose are?), but because their recommendations coax people into buying volatile stocks that directly benefit them and their firms' investment banking deals—not us, the individual investors.

Basically, stock market pundits use TV to generate buzz for their firms and to inflate their egos, and we buy into their marketing strategies because they're on TV and they must know what the hell they're talking about or they wouldn't be on TV. But, surprise, their analysis has as much to do with reality as reality TV. It's manipulated. (Sorry to burst the bubbles of fans of *Survivor*, *Big Brother*, and *Temptation Island*.) On TV, conflict—even if manipulated during editing—equals ratings. In the stock market, excitement—even if invented by analysts—equals sales. Hollywood meets Wall Street. It's the same game. We all love drama, even if it's fictional. In fact, we like it better if it's fictional. When was the last time you drove to a theater to catch a documentary?

But your investments *must* be based on trust, reliability, and real life. This isn't mindless entertainment and you don't want conflict. This is your hard-earned money that you want to grow, not dissipate from gambling on bogus advice.

That is why New York State's Attorney General Eliot Spitzer has been scrutinizing practices of large investment firms with incredible conflicts of interest issues. Due to his investigation, Merrill Lynch was fined $100 million for tying its analysts' compensation to deals that enhance its corporate clients' cash flow while encouraging individual investors to buy that corporation's stock as its value dropped like water cascading over Niagara Falls.

Although Merrill Lynch did not admit any wrongdoing (while paying its $100 million fine), it vowed to change its policies by promising that it will no longer tie its investment banking deals to the compensation of its analysts. (These analysts now presumably will have no incentive to push iffy stocks on unsuspecting investors that will benefit their firm's investing side of the business down the hall.)

In the aftermath of this lawsuit, almost all other major investment firms are vowing to make the same changes, not because they've suddenly discovered ethics or found religion but because they don't want to pay that pesky fine that was levied on Merrill.

Let's hope this bodes well for all us "little folks," so we now can get unbiased recommendations from the big brokerage firms. But don't count on it. If regulators and prosecutors trust the large brokerage firms' promise to do the right thing from now on, the brokerage firms will still be regulating themselves. Beware. The temptation of huge profits again will lure them to peek over the Chinese walls—especially if they haven't been punished for past indiscretions. (The reason we ground our kids is so they'll think twice about doing it again.)

While putting this book together during the summer of 2002, a new SEC regulation was issued that makes it mandatory for analysts and anyone else publicly commenting on stocks to fully disclose any conflicts of interest they have. The regulation specifically targets conflicted recommendations made over the phone, by e-mail, and also in the media—including TV, radio, and the Internet, which seems to have been invented to help Wall Street market its securities without the expense of direct mail.

After the implementation of this regulation, I would hope that informed investors would be more skeptical of an analyst's vested interest in a stock performance. Still, I doubt that this new requirement will change things. Given the vast sums of money involved, Wall Street's marketing gurus will surely devise ways to get around the regulations, such as burying the disclosure in the fine print of their documents or whispering the disclosure in their radio or TV commercials.

If you get nothing else from this book, understand this: The Wall Street hype found in the media—TV, radio, the Internet, magazines, and newspapers—is exactly that, hype. The hype is designed to entertain you and provide PR that will help sell lousy stocks as good investments. Think of it as bubble-vision. The bullish information encouraging you to buy, not sell, helps Wall Street sell more stocks to you. They want your money and they don't care a whit about your financial well being. They're salesmen; that's their job. If you want to build wealth based on sensible and reliable advice, *tune them out.*

Like car dealers or insurance salesmen, it's their job to sell you their products, not those of their competitor down the road that may be far better suited for you. If you walk into a showroom or watch TV, you should expect: "Trust us, buy it, then please disappear . . . unless you wanna come back to buy some more." They want you to trust them, buy what they're selling, and then go away until you're ready to buy some more. Don't expect anything more.

Have you ever bought a car or an insurance policy based on the salesmen's pitch and charisma and later sensed that he was only following this mantra: trust me, buy it, then please disappear? I have (only once, of course). You need to keep this in mind the next time you consider buying stocks from a media pitchman. Remember, these media darlings are not the independent, unbiased analysts they would like you to think they are.

Still trust the media darlings?

The truth sets you free. Use your own sound judgment to make your investment decisions, not some media star's slick sales pitch veiled as an independent analyst's tip. The latter leads you down a path paved with fool's gold.

The *National Enquirer* tabloid showcases stars and their foibles. It's amusing to browse its pages while in line to buy groceries (no one ever admits to buying a copy but somehow it's the most successful rag in America), but we don't really trust the validity of any of its stories. The stars continually claim the information is crap and most of it probably is, but there are usually enough seeds of truth in the stories to dodge legal action.

People magazine, on the other hand, is slicker and we aren't embarrassed to have it out on the coffee table when visitors drop by. We put more stock in its stories, yet the stars' publicists control most of *People*'s photos and the information that's reported. If *People* wants future access to those stars, they don't rock the boat.

Both of these publications contain a degree of spin and hype and both are hell-bent on selling us as many copies as possible. So which one is more reliable? (I prefer *People,* but neither one presents the truth, the whole truth, and nothing but the truth.) Caveat emptor. Buyer beware. You need to rock the boat if you want the truth.

The point is: Wall Street analysts, like magazine publishers and politicians, are more than willing to feed you stories and misinformation so you'll buy into their spin. The media's 24-hours-a-day financial noise and dribble drown out the big picture and most of the facts.

Are you still looking for a hero? Look in the mirror. That person's real and you can count on that person to be concerned about your best interests and welfare throughout your life.

If you grasp the basics about Wall Street and what really drives stocks up and down—supply and demand, tracking buyers versus sellers—then I have full faith that you can outshine the media darlings. Let's continue on that path.

TONIGHT'S NEWS IS HISTORY

The time of maximum pessimism is the best time to buy and the time of maximum optimism is the best time to sell.

JOHN TEMPLETON, founder of the Templeton Group

Okay, we've shot down the reliability of stock predictions from the media darlings who have inherent conflicts of interest (especially if their employers are prestigious investment banks that count on them to generate big bucks for their clients). Until they change and become more objective, don't ever let them off the hook for giving sell ratings at a measly 1 percent rate compared to their recommendations of buy or strong buy—even during a recession.

But should you trust unbiased financial news reported through legitimate new outlets—for example, when your local news anchor reports that Company A bought Company B, Company C won a lucrative contract, or Company D's CEO was fired in the midst of a scandal. After all, this information is coming from a news anchor, not a salesman. Don't make this rookie mistake. Invariably, the big institutional investors heard rumors of this news weeks before it actually played out. By the time you hear about it, the big players have already made their moves. These news programs provide a "lagging indicator." It's like getting an invitation that arrives too late for us to attend the party.

Another dark secret about the news industry is that reporters are fed a steady stream of stories by public relations agents; often, they don't research their own stories. The news media is showered with press releases, briefings, and BS by public relations agents hired to make their clients rich and powerful. A lazy reporter may change a few sentences provided to him by a Wall Street PR department and turn around and present it as hard-core, reliable news. (The same is true of the "inside scoops" reported in entertainment news.)

Often "breaking news" about the release of a company's financial report is out of date. Companies report on their performance during the previous quarter so it's intrinsically old news the moment it's published. While, the report may influence some individual investors to buy or sell their stocks the next day, the vast majority of the stock market looks ahead six months or more, not back to past performance. For this reason, most of the time, you'd be better off not looking backward either (unless the report exposes highly suspect or criminal behavior; then bail out!).

While you can't predict tomorrow's market (who can?), you can surely keep track of what's happening right now—most importantly, if there are more buyers or sellers for your stock. That's all that ultimately matters. More buyers move a stock up, more sellers move it down. Pay attention to recent trends when the stock is either moving up or down.

Remember this: Trends are your friends.

In another scenario, an investor might hear news that's seemingly unrelated to the market but he or she second-guesses what the market will do based on an inspired hunch. Consider the media hoopla that surrounded the release of the movie *Spider-Man*. When Joe Investor sees this *Spider-Man* promotion, a light bulb goes off. "Hey, Marvel Comics owns the rights to *Spider-Man* so its stock must be a great buy right now! Ye-haw, what a great stock to buy first thing tomorrow. The movie's gonna make a bundle, so Marvel will too!"

The movie was a blockbuster, but unbeknownst to Joe Investor, Marvel was paid in advance for the rights to make the movie. As a result, Marvel's stock rose before shooting for the movie ever began. Then it started falling months before the movie was released.

Bad news for Joe Investor who assumed Marvel would reap rewards from the movie's success. Again, consider news a lagging indicator when making investment decisions because, odds are, it is old news.

This wisdom from WealthEffect.com applies here.

Don't get caught up in the investment advice overload that is more likely to leave you confused than brilliant. . . . One adage of the market is that "What's obvious is obviously wrong." A little knowledge will have you chasing the herd, riding the fears and greed of the moment rather than profiting from them. Like freshmen psychology students and white belts in karate, a partially informed investor is a menace to himself and his loved ones.

To sum up, you really can't rely on the media for investment tips. The pundits are pushing stocks to benefit their investments banks and the legitimate news (given in 10-to-15 second sound bites) is too late to be of any use to an investor. It's all part of the hype machine—either to get you to buy stocks or to lure you to tune in tomorrow for more "breaking news."

You are far better off looking elsewhere for trustworthy indicators about a stock you're exploring or one you already own. Find out if there are more buyers or sellers during the last few days, weeks, or months, and whether there's a clear positive or negative trend during those periods.

3

WHAM, SCAM, NO THANK YOU, MA'AM

They could sell bubble gum to the lockjaw unit at Bellevue.

From the motion picture *Boiler Room*

No introduction to Wall Street and the world of investing would be complete without exposing the outright illegal scams and bottom-feeding perpetrators of fraud looking for easy prey.

Investing requires an element of risk. (Hey, crossing the street requires an element of risk.) But too many of us are prone to gambling fever, thinking we can make a quick fortune playing the stock market. If my neighbor Joe got into Yahoo! stock early and made a quick fortune, why can't I? This is precisely the emotion on which cunning scam artists are counting. They prey on our dreams and fantasies that one day we can be fabulously rich from an investment made on an insider's tip.

Consider this: Some fraudulent operations gross over a million bucks a month. The North American Securities Administration Association estimates that investors lose $10 billion a year—roughly $1 million an hour—to investment fraud promoted over the telephone leading to financial devastation and shattered hopes.

Let's start with traditional scams. Despite the fact that online trading has recently empowered individual investors more over the past few years, the scams found online are more-or-less the same as those that operated before. Let's not forget the insidious boiler room operations in which salespeople often sit together in a single room and pose as members of a legitimate brokerage firm. Their sole purpose is make cold calls to deceive and defraud investors, using high-pressure sales tactics to induce sales of dubious stocks and other investments.

COLD CALL SCAMS

For your sake, always presume that a stock salesman making a cold call to you is perpetrating a scam. He'll call you up, promise you a deal that's too good to pass up, and assure you that this stock will provide amazing returns on your investment. Often, the stock that the salesman on the phone is selling does perform well for a very short period because his operation or his co-conspirators are buying it to make sure it bumps up like a "one-day wonder." Then unbeknownst to you, they sell it off, and the stock crashes and burns.

Of course, the scam artist feeds you whatever lies and misinformation are necessary to get you to bite, then disappears once he has made his money, leaving you holding a very empty bag.

Here are some lines you might hear from a scam broker that should raise a red flag.

- "I've got a deal for you that's too good to pass up."
- "I have a friend who works for this company and, boy, let me tell you, they're going to be the next Microsoft in their industry."
- "You're using a telephone, right? Well, the product these guys are making is going to be as necessary to life as the phone you and I are talking on right now."
- "You'd have to be brain dead not to say yes to a deal that's this good."
- "I expect the stock to triple in value for you over the next couple years."
- "I've got an insider tip that this stock is going to go sky high."
- "Even Brad Pitt and Jennifer Aniston (or any other celebrity or couple du jour) invested a substantial amount in this."
- "This deal's so good, I'm going to put my kids through college with what I personally make."
- "You have to act *now*. A deal this good won't last until tomorrow."

They will try to entice you with every tactic available to sell you the stock they're hyping. They are even trained to become impatient and even irate if you question them too much or if you seem like you're not making up your mind quickly enough. They're counting on you to become defensive ("Yes, *I do* have the courage to invest my money"), apologetic ("I'm sorry, it's sounds pretty good, I didn't mean to be rude"), and hesitant to question their honesty and integrity anymore. They get excited when they get this kind of feedback from you. You've passed their slippery slope and become their sucker. Note that they have played on your emotions, not on your common sense. Checkmate.

By hyping a small company that either exists only on paper or is grossly misrepresented, they create demand for the stock in the market. The value of the stock skyrockets and the scam artist then dumps his own stock at its peak. The individual investors are told to hold on to their stock while the dumping continues and the value of the stock deflates until it's practically nonexistent. Pardon my French, but *merde!*

In most cases, scams of this type use microcap companies to achieve their ends. The term *microcap* means that the company has very few public shares available to be traded on the open stock market because the vast majority of the shares are held by company insiders (including our clever, despicable scam artists). The reason microcap companies are particularly well-suited vehicles for this scam is that they do not have to file annual reports or earnings statements with the SEC because they are too small. They also provide opportunities for insiders to profit when they dump their overvalued shares onto the market.

I'm not implying that all investments in microcap companies are scams. Actually, many are legitimate businesses that are trying to get into the market and deliver legitimate products and services. However, because of their volatile nature, buying into such companies can be riskier than normal because they're easy for con artists to set up.

Often, boiler room operatives give the companies that they're using as fronts for their schemes impressive sounding names and prominent business addresses in order to "legitimize" them. Be aware that the address on Wall Street may be nothing more than a mail drop for a potentially shady company. Also, telephone forwarding makes it very easy for the scam artists to hide their actual location. There have been cases where a single boiler room operation used multiple phone numbers, all coming into the same location to serve as the references you'd check (the company's bank, other investors, etc.). In doing this, scam artists can dupe skeptical investors into believing that the company actually exists and all the promises that the broker made are true. They may even go to the extent of incorporating taped background recordings to create the illusion of a hectic office. The moral of the story is that if it sounds too good to be true, it's too good to be true.

WEB SCAMS

So what about investing online? With the growing number of discount brokers operating online, more individuals are putting money into the market. The reason you get a cheap rate from a discount broker is because you're, in essence, doing it yourself. That is, you don't get advice and other perks that a traditional broker would give you, and you're buying and selling based on your own research and judgment. That being said, you're also not being pressured to buy a stock that a brokerage has an interest in selling, or so you're led to believe. Again, the bottom line is buyer beware.

Scam artists are everywhere and, in some ways, may be even more prevalent on the Web than elsewhere. The inherent anonymity of the Web perpetuates opportunities for scams, especially due to the relative low cost to distribute misinformation online. Whereas boiler room operations tend to require a lot of cash flow to set up and maintain, establishing a Web presence and promotion campaign is cheap and quick. The SEC's Web site gives a great outline on Internet investment scams at <www.sec.gov/investor/pubs/cyberfraud.htm>. In this overview, the SEC describes three tactics that scam artists use to perpetrate online scams: online investment newsletters, bulletin boards, and unsolicited e-mails commonly known as *spam*.

The use of online investment newsletters is an easy way to dupe the unsuspecting public into buying bogus stock. There are literally hundreds of sites that offer a "stock pick of the week" or other such recommendations. While some of these sites are legitimate, others only exist to be used as promotion for a stock on behalf of a scam artist.

If you look at a well-respected online journal such as theStreet.com, you can see that it looks well established and that the information is timely and relevant to those interested in investing. Scam artists realize that a lot of people heed the recommendations given by a site like this based on the fact that it looks legitimate. So you can bet that when they create their sites they will try to emulate the same look and feel of other respected sites, even down to the name.

Without getting too technical, creating a Web site that looks like another is relatively easy. You can download images from the original site as easily as saving a file to your hard drive. With a little ingenuity, you could slightly modify the files and pass them off as your own. In terms of content, there are plenty of sites that offer timely information on a variety of topics for a fee. All you have to do is embed them into your site. No one needs to know that the data is being "fed" from another source.

A glowing report for a stock posted on a site created to look legitimate could influence potentially thousands of would-be investors into buying it. Once there is enough demand, stock prices climb and those in on the scam dump their shares and run away with the profit, leaving individual investors with nothing more than rapidly failing stock.

Here again, you can see conflicts of interest coming into play. Misleading reports that make a company sound like the best thing since sliced bread are created either by the company itself or a paid promoter who has a personal interest in seeing the stock succeed. Promoters are mandated by the SEC to disclose information (such as a report that they received payment in either funds or shares, but many either bury the information deep into their site or fail to disclose it altogether).

BULLETIN BOARDS

The conflict of interest game is furthered through the use of bulletin boards on the Internet. Bulletin boards are places where people interact with one another by submitting and replying to posts that are visible in a public forum. Many people who are in the market on their own use bulletin boards to chat and commiserate with others like themselves so they can learn more about "the game." Unfortunately, because anyone can submit an anonymous post on a bulletin board, a stock insider could pose as a fellow investor and hype a stock. A post from such a source may look something like this:

Guys, SEXI is going through the roof! BUY NOW BUY NOW BUY NOW!!!!

So how do you know if someone recommending a stock on a bulletin board is a paid promoter or insider? Unfortunately, the short answer is you don't. As the saying goes there is no such thing as free advice. Either you pay for the advice up front or you pay for it later when you lose your shirt. The

SEC's site warns against investing in stocks solely based on information you gather on the Web from newsletters and bulletin board posts—especially if the company is small and thinly traded.

SPAM

Spam is unsolicited e-mail (not spiced ham) sent to you to solicit everything from pornography to stocks. Often spam e-mails involving investment scams are made to look like they're coming from a legitimate source. Because anyone can set up an e-mail account that is almost impossible to trace or even highjack a legitimate company's server resources, the perpetrators of a spam campaign can be difficult to track.

According to Jupiter Media Metrix, Internet users received about 570 pieces of unsolicited commercial e-mail in 2001. Expect that number to triple by 2006. (Unfortunately, if you ask to be removed from a mailing list, you're confirming for the spammer that the message has reached an active e-mail account. You can likely expect even more unwanted messages when they sell your e-mail address to other like-minded spammers.)

Investment spam sells the same "low risk, get in on the ground floor, get rich quick" message that most investment scams do. Through a spam e-mail, scam artists will try to get you to invest in very risky stocks using all the tactics previously mentioned: a slick Web presence, a nifty ad campaign, glowing reports from investment newsletters, and posts on investment-related bulletin boards. While most people are aware of the exaggerated claims in spam e-mails, others are investing millions of dollars in these scams because they appear legitimate.

TELLTALE SIGNS OF ONLINE INVESTMENT FRAUD

The U.S. Securities and Exchange Commission offers these guidelines for online investing.

- Be wary of promises of quick profits, offers to share "inside" information, and pressure to invest before you have an opportunity to investigate.

- Be careful of promoters who use aliases. Pseudonyms are common on-line and some salespeople try to hide their true identity. Look for other promotions from the same person.
- Words like *guarantee, high return, limited offer,* or *as safe as a CD* may be red flags. No financial investment is risk free and a high rate of return is usually accompanied by greater risk.
- Watch out for offshore scams and investment opportunities in other countries. If something goes wrong when you send your money abroad, it's more difficult to locate your money and find out what happened.
- Check out the broker and the firm. Always verify whether any broker offering to buy or sell securities is properly licensed to do business in your state, province, or country. If the person claims to work with a U.S. brokerage firm, call NASD's Public Disclosure Program hotline at 800-289-9999 or visit the NASD's Web site at <www.nasd.com> to check out the background of both the individual broker and the firm. Be sure to confirm whether the firm actually exists and is current in its registration, and ask whether the broker or the firm has a history of complaints.
- Remember, if it sounds too good to be true, it probably is!

"BOY, HE'S GOOD!"

You get a cold call. You want to hang up but the caller is friendly and assures you that he doesn't want a cent from you. You chat a bit and the caller says he only wants to demonstrate his company's research success to you by sharing its forecast of a particular stock that is going to experience a price increase. As he predicted, the following day the price of that stock goes up.

He calls a day or two later and again assures you that he's not soliciting you to invest. He just wants to inform you that his firm predicts that the price of a different stock is hitting the skids. "Our forecasts will help you decide whether you might want to invest with us some day," he says.

As he predicted, the price of the second stock declines. "Boy, he's good," you think. You're impressed. He correctly predicted that one stock would go up and one would go down.

When he calls the third time, you're anxious to make up for the opportunities you missed by not following his initial advice, and you want to invest with his firm. He seems hesitant, proclaiming he doesn't want you to make a hasty investment, but you insist on getting in on the action with his firm. You are now a full-fledged and enthusiastic client.

Now let's uncover his scam:

Our cold caller begins by contacting 200 people (including you). He tells 100 people that his firm predicts that the price of a stock will go up; he tells the other 100 that it will go down. Obviously, his prediction will be 50 percent correct.

If the stock does go up, he makes a second call to the 100 people who were given the correct prediction (he forgets about the 100 people who received the incorrect prediction). Of the 100 he calls back, he tells 50 of them that his second stock pick will go down; he tells the other 50 that it will go up.

No matter what happens to the price of the second stock, he has 50 people who now have confidence in him because he's "predicted" two stock fluctuations in a row. These 50 people are eager to invest.

Remember, he started with 200 calls and has reeled in 50 potential customers because they that believe in him after two correct predictions in a volatile market. Not bad (for him). Our friendly scammer is in a position to collect huge commissions from the 50 unlucky people he has duped.

TIPS FOR AVOIDING STOCK SCAMS ON THE INTERNET

One of the most common Internet frauds involves the classic "pump and dump" scheme. Here's how it works: A company's Web site feature's a glowing press release about its financial health or some new product or innovation. Newsletters that purport to offer unbiased recommendations suddenly tout the company as the latest hot stock. Messages in chat rooms and bulletin board postings urge you to buy the stock quickly. You may even hear the company mentioned by a radio or TV analyst.

Unwitting investors then purchase the stock in droves, creating high demand and pumping up the price. The con artsists behind the scheme then sell their shares at the peak and stop hyping the stock, the price plummets, and investors lose their money. Scam artists frequently use this ploy with small, thinly traded companies because it's easier to manipulate a stock when there's little or no information available about the company. To steer clear of these scams, always investigate before you invest.

Consider the Source

When you see an offer on the Internet, assume it is a scam until you can prove through your own research that it is legitimate. Always remember that the people touting the stock may well be company insiders or paid promoters who stand to profit handsomely if you trade.

Find Out Where the Stock Trades

Many of the smallest and most thinly traded stocks cannot meet the listing requirements of the Nasdaq stock market or a national exchange, such as the New York Stock Exchange. Instead, they trade in the over-the-counter market and are quoted on OTC systems, such as the OTC Bulletin Board or the Pink Sheets. Stocks that trade in the OTC market are generally among the most risky and most susceptible to manipulation.

Independently Verify Claims

It's easy for a company or its promoters to make grandiose claims about new product developments, lucrative contracts, or the company's financial health. Before you invest, make sure you've independently verified those claims.

Research the Opportunity

Always ask for—and carefully read—the prospectus or current financial statements. Check the SEC's EDGAR database to see whether the investment is registered. Some smaller companies don't have to register their securities offerings with the SEC, so also check with your state's securities regulator.

Watch Out for High-Pressure Pitches

Beware of promoters who pressure you to buy before you have a chance to think about and fully investigate the so-called opportunity. Don't fall for the line that you'll lose out on a once-in-a-lifetime chance to make big money if you don't act quickly.

Always Be Skeptical

Whenever someone you don't know offers you a hot stock tip, ask yourself: Why me? Why is this stranger giving me this tip? How might he or she benefit if I trade?

"Pump and dump" schemes are not necessarily organized by the company that issued the underlying stock. Frequently, the company's management is completely unaware of the reason that their previously stable stock is rising from the launching pad and into the stratosphere until they get a call from an investor trying to verify the inflated expectations publicized by the promoter.

While the majority of investment opportunities are not scams like the ones I've covered here, Wall Street's game is still stacked heavily against the individual investors like you and me. Like in Vegas, betting against the house isn't the best way to go.

HIDDEN ALLIANCES: PARTING THE CURTAIN

Why do they bury Enron senior executives at least 20 feet under ground? Deep down they are really good people.

From *The Totally Unauthorized Enron Joke Book*, by Tim Barry

The American economy is built on trust. Investing is an act of faith and faith is earned by integrity. Eighty million Americans currently own stock. While a lot of us own stocks as part of 401(k) plans, pension plans, and mutual funds, many also ventured into the stock market within the past half-dozen years to buy individual stocks. While we should all be aware of risks involved, we also should have faith that the market is trustworthy enough to abide by the rules—to play fair.

In previous chapters, however, we have learned that a little trust can be a dangerous thing. Trusting corporations to steer clear of fraud and scandal and trusting analysts and brokers for advice can have disastrous consequences. Conflicts of interest abound. But surely there must be some groups looking out for the interests of individual investors. There are, but before we get to them let's discuss one more problem.

We have developed a short-term culture in American business where executives have become obsessed with the selling price of their stock. This obsession gravitates to short-term earnings and short-term results, and our stock markets reflect that obsession. A drop in earnings of one or two pennies per quarter that varies from expectations can result in a 30 percent decline in the price of a stock overnight.

Especially during the booms, executives are under increasing and enormous pressure from stockholders to not only hit a home run with every succeeding quarterly report but to set a distance record each time that will dazzle the public—namely, investors. The lure of heady profits during the late 1990s spawned abuses and excesses. A lot of money was made, but too often standards were tossed aside. The promise of rapid profits allowed the seeds of scandal to spring up.

During 2002, it seemed that every week brought a revelation of yet more fraud—problems that were long in the making but only recently brought to light. Beyond the pervasive conflicts of interest we've explored among brokers, analysts, and investment banks, most scandals stemmed largely from accounting hocus-pocus to "manage the earnings." These scandals are driven by unrealistic expectations and the pressure to pretend that the course of business is smooth and healthy when in reality it is not.

There are, however, two independent systems in place to protect investors from financial fraud.

1. *Auditors.* Independent accounting firms provide accurate, audited statements of public companies. Their mission, as mandated by the Securities and Exchange Commission in the 1930s, is to protect the public investor from financial fraud.

2. *The board of directors.* This collective group of individuals is elected by shareholders of a corporation to provide oversight of the management of the corporation. Its mission is to be accountable to shareholders for corporate performance and the actions of the corporation.

Unfortunately, these two "independent" entities have their own conflicts of interest as they straddle the line between corporations and the trusting public. Each also has hidden alliances with corporations that present obvious conflicts of interest.

In the past, independent auditor firms were increasingly conflicted because the often served simultaneously as consulting firms to the corporations they were auditing (raising troubling questions about the footnotes listed in earnings reports, such as executives' stock options which were not included as expenses). The conflicts on boards of directors arose because these boards were too often filled with old pals and cronies who rubber-stamped anything presented to them by management.

LAW AND ORDER

Lawmakers were well aware of these conflicts of interest but had neither the will nor the incentive during boom times to stop them—especially while the Internal Revenue Service was raking in its share of profits to fill the government's coffers. Why fix what ain't broke?

Push came to shove in 2002 when Congress recognized that the investing public had had enough. Early in the year, bills were introduced during the height of the Enron scandal to mainly strengthen other controls already being put in place by agencies like the SEC and mandate harsher penalties for corporate fraud and crime (increasing the prison time for errant CEOs from five years to ten). What kicked legislation into high gear was an investigation of WorldCom that found almost $3.8 billion in disguised expenses—the largest case of accounting fraud ever. The restatement was particularly galling because the misrepresentations were not only huge but relatively simple to detect. They should have been caught. After this disclosure, 17,000 WorldCom employees were laid off.

Congress then passed the most sweeping corporate reform bill in 70 years—the Sarbanes-Oxley Act of 2002. President Bush signed it into law at a ceremony in New York City on July 30, 2002.

Instead of beating a dead horse here (and rehashing dozens of scandals involving outrageous accounting tricks that we've all heard about ad nauseum over the last year or so), I will explore these conflicts of interest as they were addressed within the context of this bill now made into law. This reform act clearly pointed out what *was* broken and badly needed to be fixed, namely the cozy and unethical relationships that corporations enjoyed with their auditing firms and boards of directors.

There is an overlap in the responsibilities of the boards and the auditors, so while the text here seems weighted towards the boards of directors, much of it applies to auditors as well. For example, a board of directors' audit committee is now the direct liaison with the auditors to improve their interaction.

BOARD GAMES

Recognizing negligence or failure of boards of directors to act independently to protect the interests of stockholders, the Sarbanes-Oxley Act of 2002 provides the following key provisions for boards of directors:

- Personal loans to officers and directors are banned
- The responsibilities and composition of a board's audit committee is regulated
- Whistleblowers are protected and given access to audit committees

Remember that personal loans to executives always had to be approved by boards, and some of these loans still reached outrageous amounts, for example, the $174 million in personal loans to the powerful Rigas family granted by Adelphia (a company which this family treated as their very own piggy bank). Fortunately, this new law bans such personal loans.

A board's compensation committee also approves salaries and bonus packages for top management. If you've been outraged by the compensation provided to CEOs while their company goes into bankruptcy, now you know who approved it. In one shocking example, Gary Winnick, founder and chairman of Global Crossing, cashed in $735 million of stock over a four-year period while receiving $10 million in salary and bonuses, consulting fees, and aircraft ownership interest. After his company filed for Chapter 11 bankruptcy (and once he finished cashing in), he pledged to give $25 million to help employees who lost money in the company's 401(k) retirement plan, proclaiming, "You can't take the money with you. The only legacy I'm going to leave this planet with is my name." I wonder how well that name resonates with ex–Global Crossing employees, retirees, and investors who suffered bankruptcies after the company collapsed.

President Bush stated at the bill signing:

Responsible leaders do not collect huge bonus packages when the value of their company dramatically declines. Responsible leaders do not take home tens of millions of dollars in compensation as their companies prepare to file for bankruptcy, devastating the holdings of their investors. . . . The pay package sends a clear signal whether a business leader is committed to teamwork or personal enrichment . . . whether his principal goal is the creation of wealth for shareholders, or the accumulation of wealth for himself.

As Bush noted, the SEC (not the current bill) requires the annual disclosure of a CEO's compensation, but that information is often buried in ponderous, confusing proxy statements seldom seen by shareholders. He challenged every CEO in America to describe prominently and in plain English the details of his or her compensation package in the company's annual report.

Bush continued by urging board members to "check the quality of their company's financial statements; to ask tough questions about accounting methods; to demand that audit firms are not beholden to the CEO; and to make sure the compensation for senior executives squares with reality and common sense."

Beyond the provisions of this bill, the SEC and Nasdaq have also proposed guidelines to improve corporate conduct and transparency, including requirements that independent directors compose a majority of a company's board; that all members of audit, nominating, and compensation committees be independent; and that all stock option plans be approved by the *shareholders*.

Note also that the new law promises protection for whistleblowers who can now report directly to the board's audit committee to assist investigations instead of having to report to management which may be a party to the problem being reported. Some critics complain that the bill is not specific enough regarding the protection of whistleblowers. They feel that whistleblowers are still too vulnerable when they come forward. No doubt there will be some cases in the near future that test this promised protection for those coming forward with potentially damaging information.

Other critics of the new law point out that Enron's board of directors *was* independent (only 2 of its 17 members were insiders—Kenneth Lay and Jeffrey Skilling) and had extensive expertise as CFOs, lawyers, academics, and former regulators. Looking deeper, however, Enron's directors had conflicts of interest because each was receiving about $300,000 annually and many had financial ties to Enron. By contrast, board directors of most companies are paid no more than $50,000 per year.

Beyond independence and expertise, a good board requires commitment and a willingness to dig beneath the CEO's presentations at board meetings so they become opportunities for the board to take a hard look at the company's actual status rather than pep rallies. The board's job is to monitor the organization, not to just nod approval. But frankly, I'm not sure how you regulate commitment.

THE BOARD'S AUDIT COMMITTEE

The audit committee arguably oversees one of the board's three most important spheres of responsibility, the others being the committees overseeing compensation and board nominations. Under the new law, the board's audit committee must be directly responsible for the appointment, compensation, and oversight of the work of any registered public accounting firm employed by the company, and each registered public accounting firm must report directly to the board's audit committee. The intention of this provision is to break up the often-cozy relationship between auditors and corporate managers by putting the audit committee squarely in between the two.

The law also states that each member of the audit committee must be a member of the board of directors, must be independent, and must not accept any additional consulting, advisory, or other fees from the company. The audit committee is also responsible for preapproving all nonaudit services provided by a firm's auditors. Which brings us to our next group.

THE AUDITORS

Theoretically, independent auditors should represent and protect the public's interest. Their job should be to dig deeper than the financial reports provided by the company and to find out what's really going on. However, you could make the point that, by virtue of the fact that the auditors are paid by the company, no audit is totally independent or unbiased. (Remember Arthur Andersen?)

Arthur Levitt, an SEC chairman during the 1990s, put it into perspective in an interview on PBS.

It's one thing for a company to pay their auditor. But that auditor has its reputation at stake in every audit that it does. The payment for the audit is an anticipated fee in the same way that paying a lawyer for his legal charges, in the same way that any service is paid for. It's when the auditor goes beyond, that and it is paid vast sums of money for consulting that I believe the audit becomes [conflicted and] compromised.

Beside putting the board's audit committee in place as a buffer between a company's management and its auditors, the new bill's authors (Senator

Paul Sarbanes, D-Maryland, and Representative Michael Oxley, R-Ohio) recognized that auditors were increasingly offering and handsomely profiting from nonauditing services provided to the companies they were auditing. This practice raises the issue of conflicts of interest because an auditor would be less inclined to question creative accounting if he or she would lose business in other areas as a result of rocking the boat.

As mentioned previously, the board's audit committee must preapprove nonaudit services provided by auditors. The new law further identifies several services that auditors will *no longer* be allowed to provide for the clients they are auditing:

- Bookkeeping appraisal and actuarial services
- Financial information systems (IT) design and services
- Appraisal or valuation services, fairness opinions, or contribution-in-kind reports
- Internal audit outsourcing services
- Management functions or human resources
- Broker or dealer, investment adviser, or investment banking services
- Legal services
- Expert services, other than tax work, unrelated to auditing

All of these services that are now prohibited presented clear conflicts of interest for auditors in the past. In 2001, for example, PriceWaterhouseCoopers received $80 million in advisory fees from Raytheon—an amount 20 times more than what it received for auditing.

The board's audit committee, of course, has the discretion to prohibit any other service not explicitly listed in the act. You might have noticed in the list above that tax services are excluded from the group of prohibited services. That's noteworthy because tax services probably represent the largest source of nonaudit revenue for accounting firms. However, to be on the safe side, some companies are already choosing to farm out their audit and tax work to different firms to avoid any conflicts.

CEO REWARDS AND STOCK OPTIONS

In the 1990s, enormous financial rewards were reaped by powerful executives, making them increasingly disconnected from the rest of their companies' employees and small investors. According to a front-page article in the *New York Times* in June 2002, the pay for CEOs rose 866 percent over the past 15 years to an average of more than $10 million, while pay for other employees rose only 63 percent during the same period.

Over the last decade, options to purchase company shares were given to top managers as bonuses or rewards and as a way to align these executives' own financial interests with those of the shareholders. Naturally, this share option is only valuable as long as the price of the common shares is rising. If a CEO had stock options for a quarter million shares, you can understand why management had such an overriding interest in causing the share price to rise by hook or by crook (pun intended).

Massive stock option grants played a major role in the breakdown of accounting practices as executives sought to use whatever means necessary, including those detrimental to the long-term position of their companies, to meet earnings and keep stock prices inflated. Stock option grants to executives were at historical highs in the late 1990s. Risky capital allocations and accounting trickery were at historical highs in the late 1990s as well. I contend that this is no coincidence.

OTHER KEY PROVISIONS OF THE SARBANES-OXLEY ACT OF 2002

The Sarbanes-Oxley Act of 2002 also doubled the maximum prison term of those convicted of financial fraud from five to ten years, as was proposed when the bill was in its early draft stages. As the president noted, "Defrauding investors is a serious offense, and the punishment must be as serious as the crime."

The same day he signed the bill, Bush also announced the creation of a new corporate fraud task force, headed by the deputy attorney general, which the president claimed "will target major accounting fraud and other criminal activity in corporate finance." He went on to say, "The task force will function as a financial crimes SWAT team overseeing the investigation of corporate abusers and bringing them to account."

According to the new law, CEOs and CFOs are now on the hot seat and are liable if they certify a report knowing that it does not comport with the requirements of the law. The punishment for fraud? Up to $1 million in fines, and up to ten years in prison, or both. Willful certifications of fraud can result in a fine of up to $5 million, imprisonment up to 20 years, or both.

The new law also accelerates the reporting of transactions (buying and selling their company's shares) by officers, directors, and 10-percent owners (shareholders) to two business days after the transaction.

In the president's speech, he took special aim at high levels of management who violate public trust.

> Corporate officers who benefit from false accounting statements should forfeit all money gained by their fraud. An executive whose compensation is tied to his company's performance makes more money when his company does well—that's fine, and that's fair when the accounting is above-board. Yet when a company uses deceptive accounting to hide reality, executives should lose all their compensation gained by deceit.

THE SECURITIES AND EXCHANGE COMMISSION

Before this bill was signed into law, the SEC, considered the enforcement agency for overseeing corporate compliance and ferreting out fraud, was understaffed and underfunded. The budget has been increased from $567 million to $776 million but has not been disbursed yet. The *L.A. Times* quotes Brian Gross, SEC spokesman: "It's really the worst of all worlds. The public thinks the agency has all the resources it needs. The reality is that not only do we not have that, but we're at last year's resource levels."

Like years past, the new law continues to put a heavy burden on the SEC to audit statements of public companies. About 130 accountants are responsible for examining tens of thousands of filings by more than 17,000 companies each year. With its current staff, the SEC cannot examine all corporate annual reports once every three years as the new federal law now requires. (These figures are taken from a report by the Senate Committee on Governmental Affairs, October 2002.)

For its enforcement division, operating in the SEC's headquarters in Washington, D.C., as well as regional offices, the SEC employs 75 accountants. According to Lynn Turner, the SEC's former chief accountant, it is not uncommon for the enforcement division to have 200 to 250 cases open at a time.

Major accounting firms assign three or four accountants full time to one fraud case, but the SEC's resources allow for only one accountant per three cases.

The bill also created the Public Company Accounting Oversight Board, comprised of five members under the auspices of the SEC whose responsibilities include investigating and sanctioning accountants. In October 2002, with a typical bureaucratic misstep, SEC chairman Harvey Pitt championed William Webster (former CIA and FBI head) to head this board. Pitt failed to inform the commission that Webster, was also a director at NextWave Telecom, a company in bankruptcy protection, as well as a member of the board of U.S. Technologies, whose stock closed at 1 cent per share as recently as October 25, 2002. Webster's 83,333 shares in U.S. Technologies, according to SEC filings, are worth $833.33 as of this writing.

Webster is now out and Harvey Pitt resigned on the nation's election day in November 2002, presumably not to influence voters who proceeded to deliver both houses of Congress to his then-boss President Bush.

THE VERDICT

As you might surmise, the Sarbanes-Oxley Act of 2002 was one *major* bill that was enacted to correct multiple sins of omission and neglect in one fell swoop. But does it lack teeth? Well, the agency in charge of enforcing the new law, the SEC, is still underfunded and understaffed.

Stay tuned to future events to see if a balance will eventually be met between these important new rules and the resources to enforce them. Or will Congress revert to relaxing regulations by loosening the reins allowing businesses to regulate themselves once again because they've "earned it." That is the typical end of the scandal cycle we explored in the first chapter . . . until a new cycle begins.

CONGRATULATIONS!

You have just emerged from Wall Street's Land of Oz. If you have passed through this field of land mines placed by Wall Street's major players (with conflicts of interest out the wazoo) and you aren't scared off yet—it's probably best if you are a little scared—then you are not only ready but you have an incentive to move on to the next step.

You get a lot of conflicting information from Wall Street. They *want* you to be confused so you're dependent on them to make decisions for you. You can drive a car without knowing what makes it run, but if it breaks down you're dependent on the repair shop to fix it. The same is true in the stock market. If you invest without understanding the basics, you may at some point have to rely on the expertise of the Wall Street players you've come to mistrust. And like at a repair shop, the less you know, the more vulnerable you are to those who want to take advantage of you.

But don't worry. All the basics you need to know are covered in the next four chapters. Take time to read and understand them. You won't be sorry.

Even you seasoned investors may find a nugget of helpful information in the next few chapters. Consider it a refresher course, if you will. (Don't be nervous. I won't tell anybody you read it.)

The last four chapters of this book lay out the criteria to help you identify great investment candidates. You will also be introduced to all the easy-to-comprehend tools you need to enable you to be a totally independent investor. You can boost your personal trading confidence dramatically with a little education and the proper tools at your disposal.

You have the power to successfully guide your own financial destiny. You can do this! I wouldn't have bothered to write this book unless I believed that.

4

KNOWLEDGE IS POWER

In most cases, knowing something is better than knowing nothing. In the stock market, however, a little knowledge gained at the water cooler can get investors into big trouble if they'll fall prey to their own primal emotions of greed and fear instead of relying on sound judgment.

Basic finance is not a required course in high schools or colleges (though it should be). Somehow, it is assumed that we will pick the subject up naturally.

It is crucial for individual investors to learn the basics of the stock market so they'll have a clear understanding of what happens to their investments. Education is key. Only then can they confidently take charge of their finances.

If your goal is to be in charge, you need to have a sound understanding of the fundamentals of the stock market. With this knowledge and a few tools that are easily accessible to you, you can succeed in the market on your own.

So what are we waiting for? Let's get crackin' by starting at the beginning.

WHAT ARE STOCKS?

A stock is a share in the ownership of a company. This means, if there are a 1,000 shares in a company, owning one share means you own 1/1,000 of the company. The more stocks you own, the greater the stake you have in the ownership of the company.

Why does a company offer shares in their business to complete strangers? It is a way for the company to raise capital. If the company borrows money from a financial institution, they have to pay back not only the loan amount but interest as well. Selling shares in the ownership of the company rather than borrowing allows the company to raise money without having to pay interest on it.

Here's an example.

Your uncle and aunt own a hardware store. Things are going so well that they need a larger store but it's too expensive for their means. To raise money for the move as well as for additional inventory, they decide to sell stock—partial ownership—in their company. You decide to invest in your relatives' business, not because you're fond of your aunt and uncle but because you think it would be a good investment because they've been successful so far. In exchange for your cash, you now own a percentage of their business's assets. You didn't loan them money (making family gatherings awkward); you bought a portion of their business.

To put it simply, this means if a company in which you own stocks grows, the value of the company grows as well. This benefits you as an investor because the value of your stocks increases correspondingly.

If you buy into a company whose stock is valued at $20 per share and it increases in value, your investment can be sold on the market at a higher price. Of course, you must remember that there is no guarantee that the company in which you buy stock will do well and provide a decent return on your investment. If the company falters or goes bankrupt, your investment becomes less valuable or is lost altogether. That being said, if you buy stock in a company that thrives, you have a chance to get more return on your investment than you would with other investments such as bonds.

What's the difference between a stock and a bond? There is an inherent similarity between the two. With both, you secure a stake in the company in which you're investing. That is why stocks and bonds are both referred to as securities. However, the similarities end there.

The biggest difference between stocks and bonds is that with stocks you get an ownership stake in a company. You don't own anything when you buy a bond. Rather, a bond is the equivalent of a loan you give to a company.

When you buy a bond, in essence, you get a promissory note from the company to which you're lending money stating the interest rate they promise to pay you on a set date when the company settles its debt to you. You don't get an ownership stake in the company because you merely loaned money to it, instead of investing money in the company.

By its nature, a bond is less risky than an investment like a stock, but, in turn, it doesn't have the potential increase in value with the success of the company like stocks. Instead, you receive a set, agreed-upon amount of money when the bond is repaid.

While this book is geared primarily toward trading stocks for personal profit, buying bonds is a safer investment if you have a low level of risk tolerance. However, safe investments like bonds forego the potential for the greater benefits stockholders can reap if the company they've invested in becomes more valuable.

This is an important concept to understand. An individual stock doesn't necessarily reflect the market. A good stock may go up even when the market is going down, while a rotten stock can lose value even when the market is booming. The daily trend of the market may have little to do with how your particular stock did that same day.

WHAT OWNING STOCKS REALLY MEANS

When you buy stocks, you own a percentage of the company whose stock you've bought. But what exactly does that mean? Does it mean that if you own stock in Ford, you can walk over to your local Ford dealer and demand a new car for yourself? Of course not. If you own stock in Apple Computers, do you have the right to call up Steve Jobs to tell him you don't like the way he's running the company? Well, you could try, I guess.

The shares you own in a company give you equity (i.e., part ownership). That means that while you *technically* own a percentage of all the company's assets and are *technically* the management team's boss, in practice, you really don't get a say in the way the company conducts its business. Well, not unless you're fabulously rich and own a large percentage of shares. What your equity does get you (proportional to your number of shares) is a small say in who runs the company by being able to vote on who sits on the board of directors. These selections are important because the board of directors of a company is responsible for making the most money possible for the stockholders.

If you don't like the way your company is being run, you can, theoretically, vote people off the board or elect new members who can change the way things are done. As I said before, though, the average investor doesn't own enough shares in a company to make a dramatic impact come voting time. The largest blocks of share ownership, and those that come with a far greater say in the company's operation are usually held by the top management of the company through stock options and by other very rich investors.

More important than voting rights, however, is the right to a portion of the company's earnings. This is where a stock's value comes into play. There are two ways in which you actually realize these profits.

The first way is by selling your shares after they have increased in value. When you own stock in a company that performs well in the stock market, the actual value of the company increases; your stock increases in value accordingly. If you bought into a company when its stock was trading at a $1.00 and it's value has grown to $1.50, you're effectively richer by 50 cents per share. This increase is only on paper though until you cash in your shares.

The second way in which stocks benefit you financially is through dividends. Dividends are paid out on an annual basis to the stockholders in order to allow them to share in the company's net income. The board of directors of a company will announce profits from which they'll pay out dividends. The stockholders' portion of this money is based on the number of shares they own, as well as the price at which they bought the stock. While dividends are usually paid out in cash, they can also take the form of more stock or even property. Most large, established companies offer dividends. The major exception to this is a high-growth company, which typically does not pay dividends. To continue its growth, the company reinvests its profits in itself to cover the costs of its growth.

Another important point about stock ownership is that while you have a stake in the assets of the company, you are shielded from its liability. That means that if a company goes under, you are not personally responsible for paying back the company's debt. This is different from a business partnership agreement, for example, where each one of the partners is liable if the partnership firm declares bankruptcy. By investing in a stock, the most you can lose is the amount of your investment.

One drawback: If a company in which you own stocks goes under or liquidates, your claim to its assets comes after most others' claims have been taken care of. You go to the back of the line and hope for the best because creditors, including banks and bond holders, get their money first. Stockholders get a portion of whatever assets are left after all the debts have been paid back.

TYPES OF STOCKS

Go for a business that any idiot can run—because sooner or later, any idiot probably is going to run it.

PETER LYNCH

While you now have a basic understanding of what a stock is and the risks involved, let's look at the differences not only between kinds of stocks but also their sizes.

Common versus Preferred

There is a big difference between common stock and preferred stock—not only in definition but in terms of how they're handled. What we've talked about up until now mostly applies to common stock.

- *Common stock.* There are no restrictions on who can buy a common stock. It is so-named because it is traded on the open market for all to buy or sell. Owning a share means owning part of the company's assets and getting a shareholder vote for each share you own. Dividends are not guaranteed, but may be paid out if the board of directors decides it's the right thing to do. However, while common stocks represent the highest potential for rewards in the market, they also are the most fraught with risk. If a company goes bankrupt and liquidates, common stockholders are paid last *if* there is any cash left over after paying back debts.
- *Preferred stock.* There may be a restriction on who can buy preferred stock. Unlike common stock, preferred stock usually doesn't come with voting rights, yet your investment is usually guaranteed by a fixed dividend for the duration of time that you own the stock. Whereas dividend payments are not guaranteed with common stock, they are with preferred stock. In addition, you're more likely to get a higher dividend than that of a common stock. Another more attractive feature of preferred stock is that you are given a higher priority than holders of com-

mon stock in the event that the company liquidates. You are guaranteed to be paid with any leftover assets before the common stockholders are. Also, due to its nature, preferred stock tends to not react as much to the growth of the company because it is sold with a fixed dividend payout.

Differences in Stocks Based on Company Size

There are also differences in stocks based on the size of the company. This is where the term *cap* comes into play. Cap refers to market capitalization. In essence, it's the total value of the company calculated by multiplying the number of shares a company has by the cost per share. For example, the cap of a company that has 1.5 million shares of stock at $5 a share is $7.5 million. This would make it a nano cap company (see the list below).

In the past, companies with larger caps were more stable and offered the highest level of payouts. However, with this stability came the tradeoff of not being able to rely on a rapid growth in value. Those traditional ideas of stability have lost their value when companies like AT&T and Enron showed us that even the "big boys" can fall.

While the delineations of cap sizes are not set in stone, the following list outlines the current standard for cap sizes:

- Mega cap: Over $100 billion
- Large (big) cap: $10 to $100 billion
- Mid cap: $2 to $10 billion
- Small cap: $300 million to $2 billion
- Micro cap: $50 to $300 million
- Nano cap: under $50 million

The large caps are the ones Wall Street tends to pay the most attention to because they are the ones over which the biggest investment banking deals are made. In general, the Dow index represents only large cap and mega cap companies. "Blue chip" stocks refer to the biggest cap stocks. Wall Street follows these companies because they have enormous market influence and staying power.

Here are the five most commonly used categories of stocks:

1. *Blue chip stocks.* These are stocks of a high-quality, financially sound company. While they offer no guarantee of investor safety, blue chip

companies tend to have long and relatively consistent histories of good earnings performance and dividend payments—in recessions as well as in booms.

2. *Growth stocks.* These are stocks of firms that usually pay relatively low current dividends because earnings are reinvested back into the growth of the companies. They are considered attractive because of their long-term prospects. Growth companies typically suffer fewer setbacks and recover more quickly from a recession than average companies.

3. *Income stocks.* These stocks pay higher dividends in relation to their market price. These companies must have steady and reliable sources of revenue in order to pay such dividends. Utilities are good examples of income stocks.

4. *Cyclical stocks.* These stocks can generate high earnings when the company is good or is improving, but suffer most during a downturn. Their stock prices therefore tend to be volatile. Automobile, steel, cement, and construction equipment companies are examples of cyclical stocks.

5. *Defensive stocks.* These stocks tend to generate higher-than-average earnings and dividends during a downturn. At such a time, investors often exhibit a heightened interest in such recession-resistant and highly stable stocks. Stocks of many utilities can be regarded as defensive because their growth rates tend to hold up in a recession.

Now that I've given you a quick tour of the various kinds of stocks out there, let's look at the different markets where these stocks are traded.

TO MARKET, TO MARKET—HOW STOCKS TRADE

> *Wall Street is the only place that people ride to in a Rolls Royce to get advice from those who take the subway.*
>
> **WARREN BUFFETT,** chairman, Berkshire Hathaway

There are two major securities exchanges in the United States, each working in different ways and representing different companies. I'd like to take you on a tour of each so you understand what actually happens when you buy or sell a stock (or bond) in one of these markets.

Securities markets deal primarily with stocks and bonds. The primary purpose of a securities market is for businesses to acquire capital from investors.

In other words, it's a marketplace—like at a mall—where buyers and sellers "meet" to carry out transactions.

One exchange is a physical location with a trading floor; the other is a virtual one (not a physical place), composed of a network of computers where trades are made electronically.

The New York Stock Exchange (NYSE)

The NYSE is what most people think of when they conjure up images of the stock market. All of those vivid scenes from TV and the movies where you see a gaggle of people yelling at each other and gesticulating wildly take place on the floor at the NYSE (or a soundstage that replicates it).

The NYSE was established over 200 years ago and is still located on Wall Street in New York City. The exchange itself does not buy, sell, own, or set the prices of the stocks traded on the floor. Using the mall analogy again, the marketplace is not itself in the retail business but instead provides and maintains the trading floor where business takes place. Like the mall management that serves as the "landlord" to the stores on its premises, the NYSE sets stringent guidelines regarding what companies are accepted (get "listed") and how these companies conduct business on their premises.

The NYSE is what is known as a listed market. That is, specialists oversee the trades on the NYSE listings between buyers and sellers for each and every stock.

The prices for the stocks are determined in an auction format, meaning that there are no set prices. It is often assumed that the closing price for the previous day is the starting price for a stock on the next day, but depending on the demand for the stock, this value constantly changes during the course of a trading day. The value of the stocks on the NYSE rises and falls depending on the amount of demand there is for each stock. When the demand is high, buyers bid higher prices in order to make sellers want to sell. Conversely, when demand is low, sellers have to lower their prices to find buyers.

The NYSE has stringent guidelines to determine which companies get listed. Only the largest and most financially sound corporations qualify for listing on the NYSE. Many of these companies are blue chip stock companies, but not all are. You even might be surprised to learn that some foreign companies are listed on the NYSE.

It is said that 80 percent of all the money traded in stocks in the United States is traded on the NYSE.

To give you a better understanding of how the NYSE works, let's go back to the role played by the *specialist*. Trades of any given stock go through a specialist in that stock (each listed stock is assigned to a single post where the specialist manages the auction process for that stock). Because all trading of a particular stock physically happens around the specialist, they have become known as "trading posts." Buyers and sellers are represented by floor traders who flock around the specialist and vie to place their bids. A trade happens when buyer and seller bids match up.

The specialist is also responsible for keeping track of the prices of the stock, and making sure that buyers and sellers are available. An equilibrium price is reached during this balancing act. An equilibrium price means that the supply and demand for the stock is very close—a few pennies' difference between the *bid* (or buy) and the *ask* (or sell) price. The difference between the bid and ask price is called a *spread*.

If you want to buy or sell a stock that is traded on the NYSE, you contact a broker who, in turn, contacts a floor trader with your request. If your buy bid matches up with a sell bid, the trade is made and each side reports back to his or her office with the details. Your broker then contacts you with a confirmation once he or she hears from the floor trader.

The Over-the-Counter Markets (OTC) / Nasdaq

Most companies issuing stocks in the United States are small and are traded "over the counter" through an electronic marketplace. Unlike the NYSE, the OTC is not a physical place. It is comprised of 11,500 computer terminals that make up the National Association of Securities Dealers Automated Quotation (Nasdaq) system. Until recently, the American Stock Exchange (AMEX) was a physical floor-based market (and the second largest in the United States), but it was bought by the Nasdaq's parent organization, the National Association of Securities Dealers (NASD), and is now part of Nasdaq.

There are three main markets that comprise the OTC: the Nasdaq stock market, the OTC Bulletin Board, and the Nasdaq SmallCAP. Of these three, the Nasdaq stock market is the most popular and widely reported.

Again, the OTC—including Nasdaq—is a virtual market comprised of thousands of computers on a network. Brokers use these terminals to get information about prices and then buy and sell securities by telephone with other brokers. Generally, the OTC securities are much smaller and have a lower trading volume than stocks listed on the NYSE. OTC is where small-cap stocks with greater growth potential can be found. That doesn't mean that all the stocks on OTC are those of small or unknown companies. Well-known companies such as Intel, Dell, and CISCO are some of the giant corporations that are content with being traded on the OTC.

Given that the Nasdaq is a giant computer network, how does trading work? OTC stocks are usually traded through a brokerage firm, which acts as a *market maker*. A market maker generally keeps a hoard of shares in a company on its own, and tends not to match up buyers and sellers with each other directly but conducts business as a middleman. In order for the system to work, the market makers continuously set bid and ask prices and, with the stocks they hold on their own, ensure that there is always a buyer and seller for each stock.

That being said, I'm not particularly fond of market makers (sometimes referred to as "Ax"). They have been known to play games with your stocks and hard-earned money.

One thing that a market maker can do to make more money for itself is to make profits on the spread—the difference between the bid and ask prices. Here's how it transpires: Once the market maker has entered a price, it is obligated to either buy or sell at least 100 securities at that advertised price. Once the market maker has either bought or sold these shares, it may then "leave the market" and enter a new bid or ask price to make a profit ("make the spread") on its previous trade.

While the market maker's profit might not seem great for each individual trade, in the course of a day, the $10 or $20 it's making per trade add up. Not only that, its making commissions on the trades from its own clients on top of its profit. Because of this, market makers are obligated by law to disclose two-sided quotes; that is, to show both their bid and ask prices.

ANATOMY OF A TRADE: THE PLAY-BY-PLAY

The chart in figure 4.1 gives a detailed explanation of how a stock is traded. It illustrates how one transaction looks from three different perspectives—those of the buyer, the seller, and the stock market professionals who execute the trade.

FIGURE 4.1 *How a Stock Is Bought and Sold on the NYSE*

 1. Roger Smith of Des Moines, Iowa, decides to invest in the stock market.

1a. Diane Whitford of Hartford, Connecticut, decides to sell 100 shares of NIKE, Inc. (NKE) stock to help pay for a new car.

 2. Roger discusses various investment strategies with an NYSE member broker and asks for a quote on NIKE stock.

2a. Diane asks her NYSE member broker for a quote on NIKE stock.

 3. Both brokers obtain quotes on NIKE from the NYSE trading floor via an electronic data-market system.

 4. Roger instructs his broker to buy 100 shares of NIKE at the current market price.

4a. Diane instructs her broker to sell 100 shares of NIKE at the current market price.

 5. The two brokers send their orders to the Trading Floor using either the Broker Booth Support System (BBSS) or SuperDot.

 6. At the post, the specialist who handles NIKE makes sure the transactions are executed fairly and in an orderly manner.

 7. The two floor brokers compete with other brokers on the trading floor to get the best price for their customers. The brokers representing Roger and Diane agree on a price.

 8. After the trades are executed, the specialist's workstation sends notice to the brokerage firms and the consolidated tape.

 9. The transaction is reported by computer and appears within seconds on the consolidated tape displays across the country and around the world.

10. Within three days both Roger and Diane are sent confirmations of their trades from their brokerage firms.

11. Roger settles his account within three business days by submitting payment to his brokerage firm.

11a. Diane's trade is also settled in three business days. Her account will be credited with the proceeds of the sale of stock, minus any applicable commissions.

(Source: The NYSE Web site <www.nyse.com>.)

HOW NOW, DOWN DOW?
MARKET INDICATORS

Definition of statistics: *The science of providing unreliable facts from reliable figures.*

EVAN ESAR, *Esar's Comic Dictionary*

"How'd the stock market do today?" If you watch the news, you can answer that question by repeating how the Dow did today (or the Nasdaq or the S&P 500). But these are indexes—indices or indications—representing a relatively small percentage of the market as a whole. A stock market index is simply a statistical indicator of how a *particular* group of stocks is performing (not the *whole* market).

The oldest and most influential stock index is the Dow Jones Industrial Average. When it is reported that the market is up or down, the reference is usually to how the Dow did that day. But the Dow represents only 30 stocks (albeit 30 of the largest blue chip American companies) and there are thousands of stocks out there that aren't represented on the Dow.

Beyond the small number of stocks it tracks, the Dow can be further misleading because it is "price-weighted," meaning that the highest-priced stocks exert a disproportionate influence on how the Dow does in general. For example, if the three highest-priced Dow stocks had a spectacularly great day but the remaining 27 had lackluster or drooping returns, the price-weighted formula might still report that the Dow had a good day. In this case, because the Dow is the main index we rely upon, we're led to believe that "the market" had a good day even though the majority of stocks actually floundered.

This example is not an exaggeration. In the late 1990s, a few giant stocks in the Dow had blockbuster showings week after week, overshadowing the rest of the bunch that were simultaneously struggling and declining but didn't carry as much weight in the Dow formula. The Dow kept going up, giving the public a false impression that all was fine and dandy on the market (because we equate the Dow with the whole market), thus prolonging the bubble and encouraging individual investors to throw even more money hand-over-fist at Wall Street.

In an article in *Financial Sense Online* titled "Why Not Dow 1,000,000?" (debunking the popular premises of best-seller titles in the late 1990s predicting the Dow would reach 30,000 or more) on November 27, 1999 (a few months *before* the bubble burst), James J. Puplava wrote the following prophetic observations about the undue influence of the "giants outshining the dwarfs" in both the S&P 500 and Nasdaq:

> [For the S&P:] This index has 500 companies—yet 10 companies occupy over 20% of its entire value. Since a small group represents a major portion of the index's value, these small handful of giants tend to move the entire index. . . . For the first three-quarters of [1999], just 11 stocks from the S&P 500 account for all its performance.
>
> For the Nasdaq, the picture is even more distorted. . . . A little more than 1% listed within the index account for 99% of its gains. Four stocks—Microsoft, Intel, Cisco, and WorldCom—comprise 25.6% of its value.

Did you notice two of those influential stocks were Cisco and WorldCom? These two were driving the boom?! I think you'll agree, it's a bit chilling in hindsight. Here's more from Puplava:

> This proportion of distortion—whereby you have the vast majority of stocks declining while the indexes are advancing—has existed only a few times this century . . . during the '20s before the Crash, in the early '70s before the last bear market, and for a short period before the October Crash of 1987.

If you own a particular set of stocks instead of funds based on indexes, as I wholeheartedly suggest later in this book, then you can essentially ignore what the market is doing and never be confused by its lopsided indications because you will not be invested in "the market." You should be invested in your own group of wisely chosen stocks and that should be the only "index" you need to track.

Again, here are the big three indexes that we hear about every day, though there are dozens if not hundreds of others.

1. *Dow Jones Industrial Average (aka the Dow or DJIA)*. This is comprised of 30 blue chip (large-cap) U.S. stocks of industrial companies (excluding transportation and utility companies).
2. *S&P 500 (aka Standard and Poors 500 Index)*. This is comprised of 500 stocks chosen for market size, liquidity, and industry group representation. They are market-weighted so the largest stocks have more impact on this index level than smaller ones.

3. *Nasdaq composite.* This index tracks approximately 4,000 mostly technology-oriented stocks and, like the S&P 500, is market-weighted so the largest stocks impact the index more than smaller ones.

Let's look at each index in depth with a more objective eye, having already established that each one is a sampling.

Dow Jones Industrial Average (DJIA)

The Dow Jones Industrial Average is an index of 30 blue chip stocks of U.S. industrial companies. The Dow includes substantial industrial companies with a history of successful growth and wide investor interest. The Dow includes a wide range of companies—from financial services companies to com-

The 30 Stocks in the Dow Jones Industrial Average

(As of this writing; with each stock's symbol in parentheses.)*

3M (MMM)	Honeywell (HON)
Alcoa, Inc. (AA)	Intel (INTC)
American Express (AXP)	IBM (IBM)
AT&T (T)	International Paper (IP)
Boeing (BA)	Johnson & Johnson (JNJ)
Caterpillar (CAT)	McDonald's (MCD)
Citigroup (C)	Merck (MRK)
Coca-Cola (KO)	Microsoft (MSFT)
DuPont (E.I.) de Nemours (DD)	J.P. Morgan (JPM)
Eastman Kodak (EK)	Philip Morris (MO)
Exxon Mobil (XOM)	Procter & Gamble (PG)
General Electric (GE)	SBC Communications (SBC)
General Motors (GM)	United Technologies (UTX)
Hewlett Packard (HWQ)	Wal-Mart Stores (WMT)
Home Depot (HD)	Walt Disney Co. (DIS)

*All Dow Jones stocks are listed on the NYSE except Intel and Microsoft which are listed on Nasdaq.

puter companies to retail companies—but does not include any transportation or utility companies which are included in separate indices. The stocks included in the DJIA are not changed often, but when they are, it's at the discretion of a committee from the *Wall Street Journal.* Unlike many other indexes, the DJIA is a price-weighted, not market-weighted, index (that is, this index does not take market capitalization into account).

S&P 500

The S&P 500 Composite Stock Price Index is a capitalization-weighted index of 500 stocks intended to be a representative sample of leading companies in leading industries within the U.S. economy. Stocks in the index are chosen for market size (large cap), liquidity, and industry group representation. The S&P 500 is considered one of the best benchmarks for large-cap stocks and accounts for about 70 percent of the U.S. market. The S&P 500's performance is considered one of the best overall indicators of market performance and the mark which mutual fund managers try to beat. Unfortunately, the top 45 companies comprise more than 50 percent of the index's value.

Nasdaq Composite

The Nasdaq Composite Index measures all Nasdaq domestic and non–U.S.-based common stocks listed on the Nasdaq stock market. This index is weighted on market value. This means that each company's security affects the index in proportion to its market value. Because it is so broad-based (with 4,000 to 5,000 mostly technology-oriented companies), it is one of the most widely followed and quoted major market indexes.

Reiteration

I want to reiterate that indexes are comprised of particular groups of stocks chosen to answer the routine question "How'd the stock market do today?" Remember, these indexes tend to be overweighted (distorted) toward the performance of the "giants" in each index, so take index performances with a huge grain of salt.

If you are invested in particular stocks of your own choosing, you are not invested in "the market" as a whole. All that should matter to you is how *your stocks* are performing.

BEARS AND BULLS: DOIN' WHAT COMES NATURALLY

Ask five economists and you'll get five different answers. (Six if one went to Harvard.)

EDGAR R. FIEDLER

Mark Twain was once asked if he thought it would ever stop raining. He replied, "Always has." The same is true with declining stocks. The slide ends, or at least it always has—and usually with a bang. After the market fell a total of 37 percent in the period between 1973 and 1974, it jumped a remarkable 42 percent in the first six months of 1975. Which brings us to the extended ups and downs known as da bulls and da bears (that's for you Chicago fans).

Simply put, a bull market is a sustained period during which stock prices are generally rising. A bear market is a sustained period during which stock prices are generally falling. What gauge do we use to determine ups, downs, and volatility in the stock market as a whole? We rely on the indicators we just covered—the Dow, Nasdaq, and S&P 500.

To qualify as a bull or bear market, a market must have been moving in its current direction for a sustained period. Small, short-term up or down movements lasting days do not qualify; these trends may only indicate corrections or short-lived movements. Bull and bear markets signify longer movements (sustained for several months to a few years) with an approximate change of 20 percent or more in the stock market's value as a whole.

Both bull and bear markets are fueled by investors' perceptions of where the economy and the market are going. If investors believe they are in the midst of a bull market, or that one seems likely, they feel confident that prices are going up. Their own confidence helps to keep stock prices rising. (Optimism is contagious.) During a bear market, investors believe stock prices will fall. They hesitate to invest in stocks, and their own concerns help to keep stock prices down. (Pessimism is contagious, too.) And pessimism can shift to downright gloom when there are as many scandals in the corporate world as there were in 2002.

Of course, the best-known bear market in American history was the Great Depression. The Dow lost roughly 90 percent of its value during the first three years of that period. More recent bear markets include those between the years 1973 and 1974, 1981 and 1982, and the one we're experiencing now (2000 through who knows when). There have been 24 bear markets in the past 100 years, as the chart in Figure 4.2 illustrates.

The longest bull market in U.S. history was the one that began in 1991 and ended in the Spring of 2000. Other major bull markets occurred in the 1920s, the late 1960s, and the mid-1980s. All of these ended in recessions or market crashes. Sound familiar?

No one said that making money in the stock market was easy. In trying times, it just takes more effort. You earn your keep through discipline, wisdom, moderation, and patience.

Investors turn to theories and complex calculations to try to figure out in advance when to expect sustained bull and bear markets—and to predict

FIGURE 4.2 *Bear Markets of the Past 100 Years*

Beginning Date	Ending Date		DJIA
SEP 1899	SEP 1900	78 to 53	−32%
JUN 1901	NOV 1903	78 to 42	−46
JAN 1906	NOV 1907	103 to 53	−49
NOV 1909	SEP 1911	101 to 73	−27
SEP 1912	JUL 1914	94 to 71	−24
NOV 1916	DEC 1917	110 to 66	−40
NOV 1919	AUG 1921	120 to 64	−47
SEP 1929	JUL 1932	381 to 41	−89
MAR 1937	MAR 1938	194 to 99	−49
NOV 1938	APR 1939	158 to 121	−23
SEP 1939	APR 1942	156 to 93	−40
MAY 1946	JUN 1949	213 to 162	−24
APR 1956	OCT 1957	521 to 420	−19
JAN 1960	OCT 1960	685 to 566	−17
DEC 1961	JUN 1962	735 to 536	−27
FEB 1966	OCT 1966	995 to 744	−25
DEC 1968	MAY 1970	985 to 631	−36
JAN 1973	DEC 1974	1052 to 578	−45
SEP 1976	FEB 1978	1015 to 742	−27
APR 1981	AUG 1982	1024 to 777	−24
AUG 1987	OCT 1987	2722 to 1739	−36
JUL 1990	OCT 1990	3000 to 2365	−21
JUL 1998	SEP 1998	9250 to 7800	−16
JAN 2000	?	11850 to ?	?

when each tide will turn. In reality, no perfect indicator has been found and I suspect it's an exercise in futility. Yet, as the graph in Figure 4.3 shows, bear markets seem to have occurred like clockwork over the last 100 years. It is such a constant that it seems like a natural phenomenon—almost as predictable as the seasons of the year.

Now look at the graph a little differently. From 1899 to 2002, what has been the overriding trend: up or down? Obviously, from this illustration, you can see that the pull has always eventually been upward.

While we're waiting for the current bear market to finish its business, I hope this 100-year "trend" showing the stock market rising over the course of time is some comfort to those who wonder if it will ever stop "raining." As Mark Twain observed, it always has. And when the sun comes out to shine again, there's no reason to suspect that the stock market won't continue to rise over the long term.

As I stated before, you are far better served focusing on individual companies and their business than the market as a whole. After all, you are not investing in "the market" but in individual stocks. While there obviously are more opportunities during bull or bubble markets, there are many opportu-

FIGURE 4.3 *Bear Markets over the Last 100 Years*

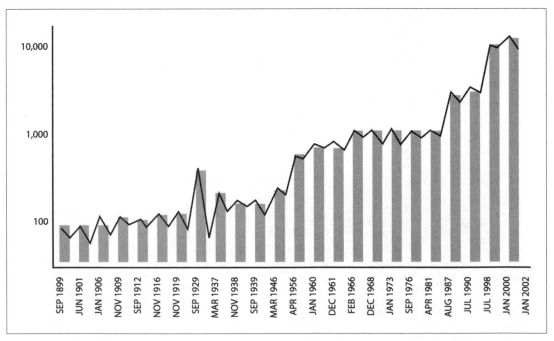

nities with individual stocks during bear markets as well. With some wisdom and the right tools to help you recognize the winners—regardless of what the market is doing as a whole—you can reap rewards whether a bull or bear commands the stage at any point in time.

RISKY BUSINESS?

People who don't take risks generally make about two big mistakes a year. People who do take risks generally make about two big mistakes a year.

PETER F. DRUCKER

No talk of investing in stocks would be complete without addressing its inherent risks.

There is no guarantee that you will make money on a stock investment. As a matter of fact, because securities aren't federally insured, you could conceivably lose all of your investment if you don't choose wisely.

Obviously, none of us wants to lose money. Yet, there is a saying that without risk, there's no gain. That definitely rings true in this case. Not investing your money will get you nothing in return. Conversely, the higher the returns you're seeking, the more risk you'll have to incur. Okay, let me pause here for a moment. I don't want to scare you out of investing your money in stocks because I believe stocks are the best investments you can make. But you must assess the risk of investing in each individual stock, or in investing in anything else for that matter.

Inflation, You Dirty Dawg

A key issue when looking at the risk/gain ratio is inflation. Basically, inflation is the rate at which your money loses buying power. As you know, $1 today is worth less than it was worth ten years ago, and it will be worth even less in another ten years. In the United States, the inflation rate has historically been about 3.2 percent per year. What this means is that even if you put your money in a safe federally insured interest-bearing savings account, you could end up losing money (not in the amount that accrues but in its buying power) if the interest rate from your bank doesn't keep up with the inflation rate. So while you might think that you won't lose anything if you don't invest money in the stock market (other than the opportunity to reap greater rewards), your cash is losing value constantly due to inflation—even while you're reading this paragraph.

Just as there are different levels of risk from mild to the mildly insane, there are levels of safety that slide all the way down to *too safe*.

But Time Is on Your Side

While the inherent risks in stock investments are higher than putting your money into a savings account, compared to any other form of savings or investments, stocks have historically offered the highest rate of annual returns over time. (If you invested $1 in stocks in 1900, you would have over $10,000 today.) So, while you might hear news of a bad day on the stock market, if you keep your money in stocks for the long term, odds are you will find that market trends that seem volatile day-to-day are not going to impact you in the long run as much as you might think. Patience usually pays off. That being said, if you put all your money into a company that goes bankrupt, you may be totally out of luck. (Okay, we got that messy bit of business out of the way.)

Here's the most important point: Stocks have outperformed any other form of investment mechanism in the long run. This is because the U.S. market has continuously had an upward trend (remember the graph in Figure 4.3?). Even through slumps and bear markets, the market continues its upward swing.

In the long term, stocks generally yield around a 10 percent to 11 percent annual return. Compare this to bonds, which are safer but usually give you only a 5 percent return. While you might think that the rate of return for bonds is attractive because it's more of a sure thing, the rate at which your money grows isn't only based on the rate of return of your investment. Inflation weighs in heavily here.

Growing money without inflation:

- Let's say you invest $100 in a stock that is performing at 10.5 percent annual return. It would take about seven years to double it to $200.
- If you invest the same $100 in a bond with a 5 percent interest rate, math dictates that it'd take little over 14 years to double the value to $200.

When you factor inflation at about 3.2 percent per year in the equation:

- Your stock investment would take nearly ten years for the *actual value* of your money to double (instead of seven years).
- Your bond investment would not double the *actual value* of your money for 40 years!

I think you can clearly see the difference in the performance between stocks and bonds from this example. If you choose an even "safer" investment that earns less than the 5 percent you get from bonds, then it would take even longer for your funds to grow. It's not hard to understand why stocks are by far the best choice for your investment to grow, as long as you take the time to research your investment and make wise choices.

But Why All the Daily Ups and Downs?

There are many reasons why stock prices fluctuate. Whether it be a general trend, a major move by large financial institutions in and out of stocks, or good old supply and demand, no one can accurately predict how a stock will perform from moment to moment. There is one area, however, that we can point to as the single most influential reason why a stock's value goes up or down: the number of stocks being bought versus the number being sold.

Buyers versus Sellers, Supply and Demand

I can't stress enough that supply and demand—buyers versus sellers—is the most important reason why a stock's price goes up or down. While there are other influences that come into play from day to day, the bottom line is that if there are more sellers than buyers, the stock price goes down; if there are more buyers than sellers, the stock price goes up. Plain and simple. (This subject will be covered in depth later when we discover how to find good stocks to buy and how to recognize which ones to avoid.)

So if the value of a stock is not based solely on the number of buyers versus sellers, then what kinds of other influences might affect it? Let's start with two big ones.

1. *Institutional movements.* When "insiders" or large corporations buy and sell vast sums of shares all at once or when mutual fund managers with thousands of clients move in or out of a stock, they dramatically move

the market with them. Each stock has a typical daily volume of buying and selling, but a major movement can be recognized as a "spike" in the volume for that day. The buying and selling by institutions occurs on a big scale and their power, by virtue of the sheer number of stocks they represent, can instantly affect a stock's value. You should also pay attention when the "big guys" jump in or out of a stock—chances are they know something that you don't. Ride the wave *with* them if you can but if you miss the boat, don't jump in.

2. *Earnings.* A publicly traded company is required by law to publish its earnings reports four times a year (once each quarter). Stocks rise and fall around reporting time when investors react to whether the company exceeds target expectations or fails to do so. While earnings affect the company's value, we saw during the dot-com bubble that some companies that never made a dollar can be represented by paper wealth that is worth billions. But when the reality set in that these companies had no earnings, their value disappeared.

Still want more? Here are some events—both external and company-related news—that *tend* to move stocks up and down. These tendencies are worth following on your radar screen but their effect is far from a guarantee of a certain result.

External events (not related to a particular company).
Prices *tend* to move *up:*

- Before a presidential election
- Before New Year's Day
- When oil prices decline
- When the rate of inflation declines
- When interest rates decrease
- When GNP reports show growth
- When raw material prices decline
- With international tensions

Prices *tend* to move *down:*

- After a presidential election
- After New Years Day

- When oil prices increase
- When the rate of inflation escalates
- When interest rates rise
- When GNP reports show sluggishness
- When raw material prices increase
- With the sudden illness/death of a president

News related to an individial company.

Prices *tend* to move *up:*

- When companies announce dividend increases
- When projections of future earnings increase
- When restructuring occurs to reduce current debt
- When an earnings increase exceeds expectations
- With rumor of a takeover attempt
- When a lengthy strike is settled
- When a company succeeds in increasing prices
- When a company is awarded a large contract
- When a company appoints a new chief executive officer (CEO)
- When cash flow improves

Prices *tend* to move *down:*

- When a company issues new shares to finance a takeover, diluting per share value
- When dividend pay-outs are skipped or reduced
- When acquisition rumors are disproved
- When an acquisition plan fails
- When an earnings decrease is projected or rumored
- When earnings decline
- With unexpected losses
- When a company is involved in price-cutting or a price war
- With labor unrest or when a major strike begins
- When a company loses a big contract
- When a popular CEO dies or resigns
- When a company's announced stock split is rescinded

Prices of stocks fluctuate but tend to follow a trend over time. They may take two steps up, one step down, three steps up, one step down, and so forth.

While making its way from point A to point Z (whether it's upward or downward), a stock price oscillates constantly. It's natural. The important thing to remember is that when you focus on the longer term, the natural tendency of a stock is to flow one direction or another.

We've now seen many factors that can influence the direction and amount that a stock moves. The bottom line, though, is that no one really knows for sure why stock prices constantly fluctuate the way they do. They just do.

Even with all their sophisticated tools, the sharks of Wall Street can't tell you for sure why or how a stock will move. Without access to these tools, it's even harder for us—the "little people"—to accurately predict what's going to happen (though computers and software have definitely leveled the playing field).

No matter how wisely and safely you play it, there will always be an element of uncertainty with stocks. The best you can do is to have a solid strategy and be prepared to deal with whatever contingencies may arise. But before we get into developing that strategy, let's finish covering the basics.

PLACING ORDERS

Until the year 2001, stock prices had been quoted in fractions for two centuries, based on a system descended from Spanish pieces of eight. Each dollar was cut into eight bits worth 12.5 cents each. (Quarter = 2 bits.)

CHARLES A. JAFFE

On Your Mark . . .

Simply put, the price of a stock is determined by supply and demand, where

- the *supply* of stock is based on the number of shares a company has issued, and
- the *demand* is created by people who want to buy those shares from the owners.

The more that people want a stock, the more they are willing to pay for it.

Now here's the dynamic that drives the prices of the stocks up or down: The supply of shares of any stock is *limited*. Investors can only buy shares of stock that are already owned (or held) by someone else. So if one person wants to buy, then somebody else has to sell, and vice versa. If a lot of people want to buy at the current price but few people want to sell at that price, then the price goes up until more people are willing to sell. When the price gets so high that buyers are no longer interested in buying the stock, then the price starts to drop.

Ready . . .

When you're ready to buy or sell, you need to understand the two prices you're dealing with—the bid and ask prices.

- *Bid (or bid price).* The highest price at which someone is willing to buy a stock.
- *Ask (or ask price).* The lowest price at which someone is willing to sell a stock.

The difference between the bid and ask prices is called the *spread.* If the bid price is $15.00 and the ask price is $15.05, the bid-ask spread is 5 cents.

So why is there a spread? Why aren't the bid and ask prices the same? The bid and ask prices are determined by the middlemen (dealers, also known as specialists and market makers) who match sellers with buyers; the spread is their profit for providing their services. An analogy might be that the middlemen are like pawnbrokers. They buy from a seller (at a lower bid price) and resell to a buyer (at a higher ask price). The pawnbroker pockets the profit (the spread).

If you want to buy, the ask price tells you how much the stock will cost you to own it. If you want to sell, the bid price tells you how much buyers are willing to pay you for your stock.

Set . . .

When you're buying stock, you also must indicate how you're paying for it: cash or margin.

The cash option is simple. Most of the time, whether you set up an account with a broker or establish one online, you provided money up front as a deposit. The costs of buying a stock (the price of the stock plus fees to make the transaction) are drawn from the cash you've already provided. No fuss, no muss.

When buying on margin, it gets much more complicated. When you choose this option, you borrow money from your broker to buy stock. Some investors choose to buy stocks on margin (with the broker providing up to 50 percent of the costs) because they can buy up to twice as many shares and thus double their possible gains. On the other hand, they risk doubling their losses.

Whether the stock goes up or down, the broker collects interest on the loan and holds on to the purchased stock as collateral. If the investment doesn't outperform the accruing interest on the loan, the investor is in a hole—even with a growing stock.

"Let me order, already!"

Once you have decided how to pay for your transaction, you need to choose the kind of order you want fulfilled. Here's a short description of the various types of orders that you have at your disposal when making a trade with a broker or online.

- *Market order.* This is an order to immediately buy or sell at the best price currently available on the trading floor.
- *Limit order.* This is an order to act when and *if* a stock reaches a specified price (the limit) or better—either an order to buy at the specified limit price or lower, or an order to sell at the specified limit or higher.
- *Stop-loss order.* This is an order to buy or sell when a certain point is reached. It is designed to limit the extent of an investor's loss (or to lock in a profit).
- *Stop-limit order.* This is an order to buy or sell at a specified price or better after a given stop price has been reached or passed. Put another way, it is a stop order that becomes a limit order after the specified price has been reached.

The following options come into play after a limit or stop order has been chosen:

- *Good 'till cancelled (GTC) order.* This is an order to buy or sell that remains in effect until the customer cancels the order.

- *Day order.* This is an order to buy or sell that expires at the end of the business day if an order has not been placed by then.

Now let's look at each of these orders more closely.

Market orders are those that are executed at the best possible price when your order is received by the trading desk. You place a buy or sell order for a stock and your broker fulfills the order as quickly as possible. Your buy or sell order is presented to the market and is fulfilled at the "next available price" which may have changed from the time you placed the order until the time your order is processed. For example, if you put in a buy order for a stock that's trading at $3.51 at the time you placed the order but the price rises to $3.57 by the time your trade reaches the market, then $3.57 is the price you're going to pay. (If you're fortunate, the price will fall before your trade is executed and you will pay less than your original order.) The same type of fluctuations may occur when you're selling your stock.

When you place a market order, your broker is obligated to move on the trade as quickly as possible to meet your intended buying or selling price to limit unpleasant surprises in price fluctuations for clients.

Market orders are the least expensive trades that you can make in terms of your broker's fees or commissions because these orders require no special attention on the broker's part. With discount and online brokerage firms, the lowest available cost per trade refers to the placement of market orders.

You will undoubtedly incur extra broker fees for all other types of orders because you're exercising more control on how the order is placed.

Limit orders are those that are executed only if the price you've specified is reached. This could mean a more advantageous price for you than that of the current market price (that is, a lower price if you're buying, higher if you're selling) should the market move in your favor before your limit order is processed. You are assured that your price won't get worse because you've set your limit; however, this limitation may prevent your order from being filled.

A variation on this is a *limit order—all or none.* This type of order specifies "my way or the highway," meaning the order has to be filled completely at the price you specify or not at all.

Stop-loss orders are those that are executed when a certain price is reached. The two types of stop-loss orders are:

1. Stop order
2. Stop-limit order

A *stop order* is entered with a price on it. When the stock reaches that price, the order then becomes a *market order* and is filled at the market price. For example, a stop order would be written like this:

Sell 200 XYZ at 50 stop

When the stock reaches 50, it triggers the order, which is then executed at the next available price, regardless if it is above or below 50.

A *stop-limit order* is entered with two prices on the ticket—the first price is the stop price and the second price is the limit price. The stop price must be reached first, then the order becomes a limit order and that limit price must then be reached for the order to be executed. For example, a stop-limit order would be written like this:

Sell 100 Shares IBM 70 stop 70.25 limit

This means that when the stock hits 70, it triggers the stop side of the order, then the stock must hit 70.25 for the order to be executed.

Some people use stops regularly and love them because they feel it's a safety measure that helps them avoid big losses when they're not paying attention. Other traders don't like them because the price may drop suddenly due to a temporary blip (like an "afternoon suck down") and the stock is automatically sold before the price has a chance to pop back up to where it was before.

As for cost of a stop-loss order, you are charged the regular commission (like a market order) and only pay extra if the stop-loss price is reached and the stock must be sold.

Two options are available *after* you've chosen a limit or stop order:

1. Good 'till cancelled (GTC) order
2. Day order

With a *good 'till cancelled order*, the trade will take place at the limit or stop price regardless of how long it takes for the price to move to that point (you purposefully make it an open-ended proposition). If you want to buy a stock at a specified price but the stock is moving slowly to get there, your GTC order means that your order is valid until you cancel it. In some cases, your broker may have an automatic shut-off limit on the length of time that an order can remain open (say 30 or 60 days), so if your GTC order hasn't been placed by the broker's expiration date, the order is automatically cancelled.

With a *day order,* you've expressed that you want your order cancelled automatically at the end of the day if it hasn't been executed by then.

Finally, these terms are also useful to know when you are placing an order.

1. *Round lot.* This specifies that your order is one in which you wish to buy or sell in multiples of 100 shares.
2. *Odd lot.* This specifies that your order to buy or sell involves less than 100 shares.

CONCLUSION

Now all you need is a method of choosing and trading stocks that consistently yields positive results. Let's move on!

5

MIRROR, MIRROR

Taking Stock of Yourself

If one does not know to which port one is sailing, no wind is favorable.

LUCIUS ANNAEUS SENECA

For the time being, let's brush aside all that Wall Street stuff. It's now time for *you* to take center stage.

In order for you to develop a financial game plan, you first need to take stock of who you are and what you want. That is, where are you coming from financially and where do you want to go? To become a fully informed investor, it is vital that you assess the "big picture" before you dive into the investment pool. Be as specific as possible in assessing the answers to the questions in Figure 5.1.

Once you have a firm handle on all of the questions in Figure 5.1, you are ready to move on to your goals.

DEFINE YOUR GOALS

Don't forget why you are investing: To enhance your financial well-being and to attain your goals. What are your goals exactly? Which of your goals are

FIGURE 5.1 *Taking Stock of Yourself*

Your Present Financial Situation (Income, Budget, Assets, Debts)

- Is your income/job stable?
- Do you have other sources of income?
- Do you have outrageous credit card debt? If so, should you concentrate on eliminating it so you're not paying all that interest?
- Do you owe money on your car? If so, can you refinance it to lower your interest rate?
- What are your day-to-day and monthly expenses? Again, be specific.
- Do you have a 401(k)? Will you be receiving a pension?
- Have you already invested in stocks, mutual funds, or CDs?
- Do you have retirement benefits on which you can rely?

Your Future Financial Responsibilities

- Are you responsible for supporting children, a spouse, or your parents—now or in the future?
- Do you own a home? Do you owe a mortgage on it? Do you often have expenses that crop up to maintain your home and lawn?
- Are you carrying adequate life, disability, property, and liability insurance?
- Do you have short-term savings that are liquid (accessible) to cover emergencies like the loss of your primary source of income or whatever other major bump in the road that the fickle finger of fate has in store for you?
- Do you have three to six months of living expenses saved or easily accessible if you lose your source of income (you'll obviously need more if you have family members who are dependent on you through thick or thin)?
- Do you have enough savings readily available so that you don't have to suddenly cash in your stocks in the case of an emergency?

The Amount of Money You Have to Invest

- Have you determined how much money you want to be liquid (easily accessible)?
- Have you determined how much money you want to allocate to longer-term investments where the money can be tied up for awhile?

Your Level of Risk Tolerance

- Have you considered the risks involved with each of your investment options?
- Have you assessed what level of risk is acceptable for you?

more immediate and which ones are projected further down the line? Once you know what you want, when you want it, and how much it costs, you can figure out how to save or invest for more immediate needs *and* how to invest in greater growth opportunities to meet your bigger and longer-term goals.

Answer the following questions to determine what's most important to you.

- If you don't own a home, do you want to buy one? How much of a down payment will you need? If you own a home, do you want to own a second one?
- If you have kids, will you be paying for all or part of their college tuition? Do you fancy going back to school yourself?
- Do you have your eye on a big ticket item like a new car? How about a boat?
- Do you need to support your aging parents?
- Would you like to take a dream vacation?
- Do you intend to live in the lap of luxury?
- Do you plan on having a comfortable retirement?

To state the obvious, it costs a lot of money to achieve these goals. To make sure that you will have enough money to finance them, I suggest you follow these two steps:

1. Make a list of your goals. Study the list and determine which ones are most important to you. Also determine which goals are short term (say, within five years) and which ones are long term.
2. For each goal, decide how much time you have to meet that goal. When you save or invest, you need to devise a plan that fits the time frame for financing each goal.

Once you have determined your goals and prioritized them, you will find it easier to choose the right types of investments that will help you to meet your goals "on time."

YOUR RISK TOLERANCE

Decide how much risk you are comfortable taking with your money. Are you a *conservative* investor, concerned above all about the safety and stability of your assets? Are you an *aggressive* investor, prepared to take higher risks for the possibility of greater returns? Or are you a *moderate* risk taker, falling somewhere in-between?

Everyone handles risk differently. Some people can live with—or afford to take—more risk than others. Other factors that shape a person's risk tolerance include their age, personality, lifestyle, time available, and inclination to oversee their own investments, and responsibilities that override any financial consideration (shocking, but there are probably some examples out there). Oh, and let's not forget the income factor, especially if there is a lack thereof.

Investing money should not be an experience that's overwrought with anxiety. If investors get anxious and lose sleep while their stocks experience natural up and down fluctuations, then they should adjust their allocation to be more compatible with their comfort level.

Determine how much risk you are comfortable with and choose your investments accordingly. I suggest you keep an open mind about stretching your own sense of risk tolerance *slightly* so you can possibly reap greater rewards.

Don't forget that while stocks may present a higher risk than other investments, they have demonstrated throughout history that they outperform all other investments across the board. Consider instead that the biggest risk for you may be not investing at all in well-chosen individual stocks.

CONCLUSION

I suggest that you seriously address all of the issues in this chapter, because they will help you reach a much clearer picture of your financial situation, your investment goals, and how much risk you are willing to assume. Knowing yourself and your situation sets the foundation for the next step: exploring investment strategies to find the ones that are right for you.

6

PICKING A BROKER
WHO WON'T
MAKE YOU BROKER

It is not enough to do your best. You must know what to do and then do your best.

W. EDWARDS DEMING

One of the most important investment choices that you will make is picking a broker that meets your goals and needs. You have a right—no, an obligation—to choose the right broker. Never forget that it's your money. If you feel the least bit uncomfortable in establishing a relationship with a particular broker, look elsewhere.

In the beginning of this book, we explored the great Wall Street melodramas with a cast of characters so caught up in their conflicts that they wound up disregarding the individual investors. In our story, that's you.

I think it's abundantly clear that you're better off controlling your own destiny rather than constantly sidestepping all the land mines of confusion and misinformation planted by the big boys in the financial world. To control your own financial destiny, you only need to be armed with the knowledge and tools to make sound investment decisions on your own.

However, even with the proper street smarts, the system is set up so that there's one entity we must all deal with. If you want to invest in stocks or bonds, you have to go through an intermediary. There's no getting around it. You *cannot* execute trades on your own (unless you happen to be a licensed broker).

WHAT EXACTLY IS A BROKER?

If you want to buy or sell stocks, you need to use a licensed broker. The term *broker* can refer to an individual or the brokerage firm as a whole. In either case, each one provides the essential service of linking individual investors with the financial markets.

As an individual, a broker (also known as a stockbroker) works for a brokerage firm. He or she serves as the sales agent who recommends investments and executes investors' orders. Brokers serve as intermediaries between those who want to buy and those who want to sell. In addition to their salary, they make their living from commissions or fees for the sales and deals they make.

Let's be very clear. Brokers are salespeople. Never forget that. Caveat emptor. Buyer beware. I am not knocking brokers just because they are in sales; some of my best friends are salespeople (hey, I was one myself for Motorola). Deep down, most stockbrokers are decent people, but just like car salespeople, real estate agents, and insurance agents, they make their living by making sales—by taking people's money when they sell a product or service—not by sending you home empty-handed.

Brokers have little incentive to teach us to become self-sufficient because they lose commissions if we don't follow their advice. They count on customers to be blissfully ignorant. That way, it gives them a lot more leeway to screw up if we're too clueless to know better. Our naiveté gives the less scrupulous brokers the power to manipulate us into making unwise investments. (Remember, the Wizard of Oz was a heckuva lot more powerful before Toto pulled back the curtain to expose him as the scam artist he really was.)

The moral of this story is the more you understand about the market and its products (whether it be stocks or cars or insurance), the more the power shifts from the salesperson back to you. Instead of allowing the broker to second guess you, you can second-guess the broker's recommendations, and you should—every single time. Especially because a broker's mantra is often "buy, buy, buy" and seldom "sell."

RULES OF ENGAGEMENT

A stockbroker in the United States must pass two licensing examinations given by the National Association of Securities Dealers (NASD). These exams (called Series 7 and Series 63) certify that a broker understands everything about what he or she is selling to you as well as all the pertinent regulations and laws in the securities industry. After passing these exams, a broker is licensed to advise you on investment choices, solicit business from you, and execute transactions on your behalf. (Brokers may do some research on their own but officially they are *not* research analysts.)

By law, all licensed brokers—individuals and firms—are members of NASD and must abide by its rules and regulations. As of June 2002, there were about 5,500 member firms registered with the NASD, along with 91,100 branch offices, and 678,600 registered representatives. If you ever want to check liscensure of a prospective or current broker, you can go to NASD's Web site <www.nasd.com> and check the database as part of its public disclosure program.

All brokerage firms must adhere to the Securities and Exchange Commission (SEC) rules as well as the exchange and over-the-counter rules. Only exchange members (e.g., New York Stock Exchange members) are permitted to execute orders on the floor of an exchange. To become a member of an exchange, a brokerage must buy a "seat." The recent going rate for a seat is about $500,000 (depending on supply and demand, of course). Firms not owning seats are called nonmembers. Their orders for exchange-listed stocks must be processed through a member firm. Without that connection, they can only execute orders in over-the-counter markets.

SIMPLY SPEAKING

Before we move on, let's review the basic ABCs of how a client opens an account with a broker and places an order. Placing an order online is a little different, but the process is *virtually* the same (pun intended).

- The first step is choosing a broker.
- Once you have selected a broker, you open an account by signing an agreement and depositing money with your broker which you will use to buy securities in the future.

- When you decide to buy stock, you contact your broker and place an order. The broker provides you with the current trading price of the stock you want. You confirm how many shares you wish to purchase. To be certain, your broker asks if you're ready to execute the order (on-line, you get a prompt on your computer asking you to confirm). If you respond in the affirmative, your order is executed.
- Your account is then debited for the price of the stock at the time of the transaction multiplied by the number of shares you bought, plus the broker's commission. If you don't have enough cash in your account to cover the full cost, the broker sends you a bill that you must pay within three business days.

Before shopping around for a broker, you will be far better prepared to choose one if you have already determined your financial goals and objectives and prepared a personal financial profile including your income and assets, your debts and obligations, and your risk tolerance. (These issues were explored in Chapter 5.)

The spectrum of firms available to you is vast. Some firms have huge research departments, others specialize in particular types of companies, and others essentially serve as order takers. Generally, the more guidance you need from a broker, the higher the broker's fee.

Later in this chapter, we'll compare the major types of brokerage firms from which you can choose and explore the relatively new phenomenon of online trading. But first, let's finish covering the basics that pertain to all brokerage firms.

COSTS

Trading fees aren't the only costs associated with brokerage firms. You need to explore the following before being able to make a fully informed decision about the cost of doing business at any firm (every brokerage has different terms and conditions for opening an account):

- What is the minimum deposit or balance needed to open the account? (This ranges from thousands of dollars to nothing.)
- What other costs are involved in opening an account? Are transfer fees applicable if you already have a broker?

- What are the maintenance fees associated with the account and how often will they be assessed?
- Is the commission truly a flat rate or are there different rates depending on whether the trade is a market order or a limit order? (See Chapter 4 for an explanation of the different trading options available to you.)
- Are there extra costs associated with high-volume trades?
- Are discounts available for active traders?
- Are there fees for inactivity or penalties for not maintaining a minimum balance?

FOLLOW-UP QUESTIONS

Once you've narrowed down your selection to a few brokers, you should talk with each broker in person or on the phone (unless the brokerage is strictly online). Make sure you get along with the financial professional. Also, make sure that he or she understands your goals and risk tolerance.

The SEC suggests you ask the following questions before hiring an investment professional. (If you are not comfortable asking all of these questions, you can verify most of this information online; see the sidebar about the SEC and NASD Web sites for more information.)

- What experience do you have, especially with people in my circumstances?
- Where did you go to school?
- What is your recent employment history?
- What licenses do you hold? Are you registered with the SEC, the NASD, or any individual states?
- What products and services do you offer?
- Can you only recommend a limited number of products or services to me? If so, why?
- How are you paid for your services? What is your usual hourly rate, flat fee, or commission?
- Have you ever been disciplined by any government regulator for unethical or improper conduct?
- Have you been sued by a client who was not happy with the work you did?
- For registered investment advisers: Will you send me a copy of both parts of your Form ADV? (Part 1 of the ADV has information about the

advisor's business and whether they've had problems with regulators or clients. Part 2 outlines the advisor's services, fees, and strategies.)

BEFORE SIGNING ON THE DOTTED LINE

Three critical decisions must be made and spelled out in the application agreement before you sign it:

1. Who will control decision making regarding your account? (It should be you unless you give discretionary authority to the sales rep.)
2. How will you pay for your investment? (Will you maintain a cash account or will you open a margin account?)
3. How much risk will you assume? (You specify your overall investment objective in terms of risk.)

When establishing an account online, the broker may need you to mail completed application form with your signature.

Here's an important alert from NASD: When opening a new account, the brokerage firm may ask you to sign a legally binding contract to arbitrate any future dispute that you may have with your broker, meaning you cannot sue them. However, federal securities laws do *not* require that you sign such an agreement. If you don't sign the agreement, you still may opt for an arbitration process to settle a dispute for damages; but signing such an agreement

For More Information

For additional information about checking out brokers and advisors, visit the SEC Web site at <www.sec.gov/investor/brokers.htm>. Also, you may investigate your prospective or current broker at the National Association of Securities Dealers (NASD) Web site at <www.nasd.com>. Virtually every broker/dealer in the United States that conducts a securities business with the public is required by law to be a member of NASD. If you have problems or complaints relating to a broker, contact NASD's dispute resolution forum either online or by phone toll-free at 800-289-9999.

The NASD Web site also lists prohibited conduct by brokers.

means that you give up the right to sue your broker and the firm in court. Remember, you have the right to refuse to sign this agreement.

THE NITTY GRITTY

An economist is an expert who will know tomorrow why the things he predicted yesterday didn't happen today.

LAURENCE J. PETER, author of *The Peter Principle*

Now let's get down to the nitty gritty of how to choose a broker that's right for you. Then we'll explore the relatively new phenomenon of online trading.

Two Major Brokerage Types

To narrow the field, let's look at the two major types of brokers from which you can choose:

1. *Full-service broker.* This type of broker costs much more, justified by their advice based on the firm's research and analyst reports, claims to offer clients greater access to initial public offerings (IPOs) because their firm has investment and underwriting branches, solicits business, and is paid mostly by commission—meaning they're compensated not according to how well your portfolio performs but how often you trade. (Examples: Merrill Lynch, Morgan Stanley Dean Witter, Salomon Smith Barney.)
2. *Discount broker.* This type of broker charges quite a bit less because you typically research and choose investments by yourself, though discounters now offer more research online and personalized attention than in the past. Discount brokers usually don't solicit business, charge clients fees instead of commissions, and makes money by doing business in volume, counting on their lower prices and reliability to generate more trades. (Examples: Fidelity, Charles Schwab, Waterhouse Securities.) A subset is the *deep discount broker* for large-volume transactions; these offer rock-bottom rates with no customer support.

Online firms also come in two varieties: firms with offices enabling face-to-face or phone interaction, and virtual firms with no physical presence. I'll address investing online later, but first, let's continue with the two main kinds of brokers—full-service and discount.

The most obvious differences between a full-service and a discount broker are:

- The level of customer service and personalized advice (more is offered by full-service brokers but discount brokers often have better and more intuitive Web sites)
- Whether the price per trade is based on commissions or fees

Okay, let's look deeper into these brokerages and their differences.

Full-Service Brokers

Full-service brokerage firms charge much higher commissions that they justify with the benefits they provide, such as a responsive customer service department, account management options (e.g., providing credit cards and money market funds that you can use as a checking account), and insider advice on stocks from their brokers based on research reports prepared by their in-house analysts.

Large firms have vast resources to hire "star" analysts who research the past performances and assess the future prospects of companies (especially ones that are clients of their firm's investment banking department). Their brokers pass the golden tidbits from these reports on to their individual customers. In essence, you pay a higher commission for the expertise that comes from their advice. Of course, *if* the advice is sound and free of conflicts of interest, the higher fees may be worth it. After all, the advice you're getting from your broker is based directly on that of analysts who have diplomas boasting MBA degrees from prestigious business schools.

Notice that I emphasized *if* they could guarantee that their advice is sound and free of conflicts of interest. But this is rarely the case in a large brokerage house because the broker's advice is based on the assessments of their in-house analyst who's under duress to please corporate clients with buy recommendations. Earlier, we explored why analysts' advice is so tainted. When the Chinese walls were in place, departments were supposed to be disciplined enough not to "cross the line" into each other's business, but we discovered that those walls came tumbling down, so we know their research is biased. The ones channeling the analysts' recommendations are the firm's brokers who serve as the individual investors' lifeline to the firm.

If an analyst's job is now akin to that of a lawyer—an advocate for his client—then the broker can be likened to a car salesperson. To carry the analogy further, it's the broker's job to smooth-talk you into buying a car off the lot. If you buy any car on the lot, the broker and the dealership get a commission, but if you can be steered instead to buy the car manufactured by their most influential client, then *all* the parties on their side benefit. Ultimately, it's of little concern to the firm that you wind up with the best car for your needs, as long as they've dazzled you enough to make the purchase they wanted you to make. Insert "stock" instead of "car" in this paragraph and you get the idea.

The reason why the recent Merrill Lynch scandal erupted is not because analysts gave favorable recommendations to stocks that they acknowledged in e-mails as "pieces of crap," but because their brokers relayed those glowing recommendations to their trusting customers. Subsequently, individual investors lost billions of dollars with bogus stocks while the firm got rich off huge commissions from their investment banking clients. Given that full-service firms invariably have an investment-banking branch, it's impossible for full-service brokers to avoid this conflict of interest because it's built into their system.

Let's look at another "plus" that a full-service brokerage offers to individual investors. Because these firms have investment banking branches, their brokers are much more aware of IPOs because their firm's are often the ones initiating them. In theory, this means that you have an advantage as a customer because you're in a position to get tipped off when one of the firm's corporate clients goes public and its stock is initially offered at a very low price. Early-bird buyers get in on potentially great investments before the price skyrockets. But do you really have an advantage? Well, if you get first dibs like their preferred customers do, you can make a killing along with the firms themselves. But do you think you'll get the same heads-up call about an IPO as a powerful deep-pocketed institutional investor who can buy hundreds of thousands of shares? Let me put it this way: No.

Remember that table in Chapter 1 that listed the buy and sell recommendations of analysts at the major firms (7,033 buy to 57 sell recommendations). Because of conflicts of interest between their departments, it is in their interest for you to buy stocks *after* the IPO ship has sailed and for you to hold on to those stocks even as the company tanks to keep their corporate clients happy to the bitter end. If brokers ever told you and the masses to sell, they would offend the corporate clients and lose their business. They can't afford to lose business from their corporate clients, but they can afford to lose yours.

Through salaries and bonuses, the firm makes it clear that an analyst who pleases corporate clients rather than alienates them will go much further than a straight shooter. This brings us back to the broker whose job it is to relay the analyst's recommendations to you. Like analysts, brokers in a full-service firm make their money through commissions and bonuses for selling you "prime" stock (prime to *them*), or convincing you to sell some of your best stocks so you'll have cash available to buy something more to their liking. By doing this, they are scratching a client's back while raking in another commission on your new buy. While brokers at any firm have incentives to boost their sales, the recommendations of those in the full-service firms carry more weight because their firms are thought to offer "insider" information from their research reports and the opportunities to get in early on IPOs. Yet these promises don't always pan out.

Let's not forget the effect these higher commissions you pay to full-service brokers will have on your investments. If you pay $150 commission on a $1,000 stock purchase, your investment will have to earn 15 percent just to cover the commission you paid.

In order to compete with the popularity of discount brokers, full-service brokers now offer *wrap accounts* in which a broker manages an investor's portfolio in exchange for a flat quarterly or annual fee (about 1½ percent of the account's value). This fee covers management expenses and commissions for an *unlimited* number of trades—as many trades as you and your broker want to make. If you have an especially active account, a wrap account can bring the cost down on a per trade basis closer to that of the discount firms. The wrap also eliminates a broker's incentive to rack up commission fees because all trades are paid for up front; therefore, the broker only trades when it is advantageous to you. (A wrap account often requires an initial investment of at least $50,000 to $100,000—hey, the brokerages have to make sure that your the 1½ percent fee based on the value of your account isn't chickenfeed.)

If you go the full-service route, you might also ask about another type of account that they may offer where their fee is based upon the *value* of your account—therefore, it is directly tied to how well your account is performing. With this kind of account, the broker's incentive is to increase your account's value because that's how they make money.

Discount Brokers

Discount brokerage firms function on a different business principle than their full-service counterparts. Instead of commissions, discount brokers usually charge flat-rate fees with trades costing anywhere from a third to a fifth of what a full-service firm charges. For example, Fidelity's fee on a per-trade basis starts as low as $14.95. Due to a discount firm's lower costs per trade and lower account maintenance fees, you get fewer perks, little or no financial advice, and far less customer service than with the full-service firms.

Another big difference is that discount brokers do not have investment banking branches and few, if any, corporate clients, each of which dominates the full-service firms' conflicted interests. Also, individual brokers at the discounters are often paid a flat salary for their work (with bonuses more often based on results of offering good stock tips that benefit their core clients—individual investors), and therefore do not have the incentive to push some stocks over others. In other words, there's less bias involved.

Based on these two facts alone—lower fees and less likelihood of conflicts of interest—discount brokers should be more attractive to you than the full-service variety.

There is a subclass of discount brokerages known as *deep discount brokers*. Basically, these firms offer the lowest prices per trade with even fewer frills. A deep discount broker might be a good choice for those making a high number of trades per month (i.e., for day-traders as opposed to investors), however, if you make a moderate number of trades per year, then the cost per trade should only be one of your considerations. A discount broker is often a better choice because they offer some degree of customer service should you need to call about a problem or occasionally want to meet face to face at a branch office (and they're more likely to be well-established than some deep discounters might be).

Deep discounters conduct their business exclusively online to keep their overhead down.

The point of this book is to empower you as an investor (with an obvious emphasis on stocks) so you can take charge of your financial destiny. I want you to establish a comfort level to make most, if not all, of your investment decisions. Therefore, you don't need a full-service broker if you are capable of making your own choices.

When shopping for a broker, you're likely to hear disparaging and condescending remarks about discount brokers from the big full-service guys.

While it is true that you'll get a lot more hand-holding from a full-service firm, I don't think that it's worth the cost or the risks of being led down a primrose path.

Eeeny Meeny Miney Mo: Full-Service or Discount?

For investors who have a solid understanding of the market, feel confident that they can conduct their own research, have the tools available to recognize solid stock choices, and have a few hours each month to devote to controlling their financial destiny, I strongly suggest that they bypass the big commission and conflicted advice from a full-service broker.

If this profile describes you (and it should with the aid of this book), then the discount broker model was built for you: You can trade online and still have customer service at your disposal when you need it. Remember, a discount broker's customer service people do not pick stocks for you. They are there to answer questions and solve problems that may arise.

Trading Online

Trading online refers to the method of placing orders via the Internet to buy and sell securities, including stock, instead of placing orders by communicating directly with a broker by telephone or in person.

Though most full-service brokerages now have online capabilities, their costs for trades are invariably higher than those of discount brokerages because discounters generally only charge for services that you use. From now on, when talking about online investing I will be referring to discount brokers because they offer lower cost per trade and less reliance on recommendations and customer services.

Before we discuss online trading, I must warn you about the temptation to "overtrade" by trading too frequently or impulsively without considering investment goals or risk tolerance. Overtrading can affect investment performance, raise trading costs, and complicate your tax situation. It's empowering to have the ball totally in your court but be aware that with freedom comes responsibility.

Many online brokerages offer research tools. Some larger ones even have their own analysts and researchers who post reports about companies or market sectors. Because discount firms theoretically have no corporate clients to impress, there's a higher likelihood that their recommendations are less biased. That being said, any report posted by online brokers should not be used as the sole determining factor in your investment decision. But if tools are made available online, you may as well utilize them and take their recommendations with a grain of salt.

If you're a highly active trader, you should explore if there are discounts available to you, or if there are account options offering you a better deal. Some accounts charge a monthly fee instead of a per-trade rate.

Also, remember that the lowest per-trade cost advertised is almost always for market orders (see Chapter 5). If you want to place a stop or limit order, expect the price to be higher. The reason for this is simple: orders other than market orders require more attention from a broker, and therefore higher prices are charged.

When shopping around for an online broker, you'll come across many different deals and packages available, as well as varying initial deposit amounts required. You should take the time to look at various options and choose the one that suits your needs.

I won't recommend any particular online brokers in this book (I have preferences but my objectives and needs are different from yours). Also, I want to assure you that I have no ulterior or financial motive to recommend one online broker over another. Instead, I'll refer you to three independent Web sites that are either affiliated with the government (SEC and NASAA) or obligated not to show preferential treatment because it represents all brokerage firms (NASD). These Web sites not only offer great articles and tips about online trading, but they also provide links to other sites that offer independent ratings and rankings of online brokerage firms.

- SEC (Securities and Exchange Commission): <www.sec.org>
- NASAA (North American Securities Administration Association): <www.nasaa.org>
- NASD (National Association of Securities Dealers): <www.nasd.com>

Some of the links on these sites will take you to other sites that offer comparisons of different firms' testimonials and user reviews. While I would never rely on the validity of a company or broker purely based on user reviews (remember online message boards can be manipulated and corrupted), the services that offer these comparisons can be valuable tools to use when shopping for a broker. For example, one site rates brokers based on a dozen objective criteria such as ease of use, customer service options, track record, and costs to the consumer.

Before signing up for an online brokerage account, you need to make sure you understand exactly what customer service options are available to you. Can you call up the brokerage and ask an actual person questions on technical or trading issues? How responsive was that person? Does the firm offer you a way of placing trades over the telephone as well as online in case its network goes down or you don't have access to a computer? (If you need to sell stocks ASAP for whatever reason, the last thing you need is a computer glitch or not have access to a computer when the trade is urgent.)

Once you've chosen an online broker, you'll need to sign up for an account. While some brokers seem to offer immediate access online, most require that you send financial information with a signature and a check for the initial deposit amount before you can actually begin trading. This process can take a little time, so be aware that, in most cases, you can't just sign up and begin trading the same day.

The process of making a trade is fairly straightforward. Once you have an account, you use funds within your account to buy stocks of your choice (or have funds added to your account when you sell stocks). All you have to do is select the stock you want to buy or sell, the number of shares, and the type of order (e.g., market or limit).

After you've submitted your trade, wait to receive a confirmation. If you do not receive one immediately, do *not* resubmit the order. It is possible that there's just a delay in the server giving you a response. If you inadvertently place a duplicate order, you might end up buying twice the number of stocks you wanted. The same applies to waiting a sufficient amount of time to ensure that a cancellation was submitted; give it a chance to go through.

When trading online, you need to be especially vigilant when buying or selling highly volatile stocks. Because online trading isn't automatically processed (contrary to many people's beliefs), by the time the order gets routed to the floor of the NYSE or through the order processing network of one of the other markets, the price that was quoted at the time of your order may be different from the current price. Unless you place a limit order, the price is not guaranteed. While the broker is under an obligation to perform "due diligence" in processing your order as quickly as possible, there is no guarantee you will be granted the price rate that you saw quoted online.

Also be aware of the hours during which the firm will actually execute orders for you. While you can submit orders through most online brokerage firms 24 hours a day, if the market is closed at the time, your order will not be placed until the next business day. For example, orders can only be processed at the NYSE between 9:30 AM and 4:30 PM Eastern time. However, markets offering "after hours" trading (often referred to as "futures") such as Nasdaq and OTC (over the counter), your trade can go through a couple hours *before* and *after* traditional NYSE hours.

Behind the Scenes of Your Online Stock Trade

Online trades are not handled automatically at the bat of an eyelash. Remember earlier in this chapter when I told you that one has be a licensed securities trader to place an order? While it seems like you're placing an order directly with the market itself when you're trading online, the order still has to go through a broker (a real human and his or her computer). Figure 6.1 gives you a play-by-play example of what happens when you place an order online. As you can see, the trade doesn't happen instantaneously.

Another thing to look out for when shopping for a trading firm is how it confirms your order. Make sure the firm's notification policy is understandable and serves your needs. Depending on how your online broker works, you may not get a clear indication that your order has gone through. If you go ahead and resubmit the order, you may actually be placing multiple orders. As I stated earlier, you may end up multiplying your order if you resubmit.

FIGURE 6.1 *How an Online Order Is Placed*

You submit an order for shares of Coca-Cola stock.
↓
The order is received by the brokerage firm and routed to your representative.
↓
Your broker takes the order and places it electronically, as soon as possible, with the NYSE.
↓
The brokerage firm's representative on the floor receives the order and places the order with the specialist handling Coca-Cola.
↓
The trade is made and your firm's representative sends a message back to your broker.
↓
You get confirmation from the brokerage firm that the trade was successful (or notice of a problem) along with the details of the trade (shares traded, time of execution of the trade, cost to you, etc.).

You need to remember that when you're trading stocks that are volatile and moving quickly, the prices might be dramatically different in the market by the time your order has been routed there. As long as you understand this and you make effective use of limit and stop orders when needed, your online trading can be executed as you intended.

As I suggested earlier, if you need outside help when the stakes are high or you want to make sure you're putting together a well-rounded portfolio, then by all means seek guidance. But instead of paying an expensive full-service broker year-round to be available if and when you might have questions, you can hire an independent analyst or financial planner and pay them on an hourly basis to gain their unbiased advice on any particular problems you're having. You can pay the advisor a one-time fee (hopefully he or she was very helpful) and that's the end of it.

OVERVIEW AND OBJECTIVES

Risk comes from not knowing what you're doing.

WARREN BUFFETT, chairman, Berkshire Hathaway

In this book's introduction, I listed the objectives that any individual investor should embrace to become an independent and successful trader. So far, I have covered two major areas and their intrinsic objectives:

1. Identifying institutions that are inherent players in the stock market and the pitfalls in dealing with those players due to their conflicts of interest
2. Understanding the ABCs of investing and trading

Though these two areas will be revisited, we're now ready to focus on the next topic: Learning about the criteria and tools to confidently choose your own investments—namely, stocks.

In the last portion of this book, I will concentrate on the following objectives that pertain to identifying stocks to buy, sell, or put on your radar screen for future consideration.

- Taking the guesswork out of trading stocks
- Grasping what really drives stocks up and down

- Knowing what criteria to look for to identify great opportunities
- Making trading choices simply, quickly, and reliably
- Pinpointing entry and exit signals (when to buy and sell) for your trading style
- Increasing your profits and stopping your losses
- Establishing a method of trading that yields consistent positive results
- Managing your stock portfolio in minutes per day
- Making money in bull *and* bear markets

Let's go for it.

7

THE GENESIS OF WIZETRADE™

New Approaches in a New World of Investing

Learning is about more than simply acquiring new knowledge and insights; it is also crucial to unlearn old knowledge that has outlived its relevance. Thus, forgetting is probably at least as important as learning.

GARY RYAN BLAIR, president, GoalsGuy Learning Systems

In the mid-1980s, I worked in sales for Motorola where my father was a manager. I vividly remember my father telling me, "If you take care of the customer, the customer will take care of you." At the time, I was young and just trying to make rent, and, frankly, I was more concerned about taking care of myself than my customers. Fortunately for the customer, I was selling quality Motorola products. I was out for myself first and foremost, so I never paid much attention to my father's advice.

However, when I became an entrepreneur—owning a brokerage firm and now running an investment software company specializing in service after the sale—my father's advice not only made sense but resonated with me. Satisfied customers *do* take care of you and help you succeed. They not only provide you with business but they refer their friends to you as well. My father's advice was so basic and ingrained in me now that I'm continuously amazed that so many companies just don't get it.

The investment software I created is Wizetrade™. For the rest of the book, I will be using the easy-to-read charts from Wizetrade™ for examples and illustrations. After all, I personally developed Wizetrade™ with *all* of the objectives for successful trading by individuals in mind that I listed in the previous chapter.

I want it to be clear that by using Wizetrade™ for illustrative purposes in this book I am not trying to sell software to you. My goal is to empower you to invest and trade on your own, regardless of what tools you use. After all, you bought this book—not the software—so I'm trying my best to offer great service to you, the "customer," in that capacity. This book is meant to be of great value to you whether or not you have the Wizetrade™ software. This book will pave the way for you to confidently make successful investments.

The old methods of investing don't work anymore. They had their place before the information and computer age, but today investing is actually more simplified: It's about buyers versus sellers. Knowing this everything else falls into place. Wizetrade™'s charts simply help me to illustrate this point and show you how you can achieve all the other objectives for successful trading that I have laid out.

If you take from this book the theory and belief of supply and demand along with the knowledge that will allow you to be a confident and independent investor, then my mission has been successful.

When I owned my brokerage firm, I was very frustrated watching my customers lose money. It was agonizing to see individual traders—my clients—getting devastated in the marketplace with little reliable guidance from brokers and analysts. (These customers were hardly in the mood to "take care of me.") I wanted to provide far better service than that. However, my Wizetrade™ software didn't just magically pop up one day in a box.

HOW WIZETRADE™ WAS DEVELOPED

Before I ever owned a business, my early investing experience involved losing about half of my own portfolio with a broker. So I wasn't too excited when my two brothers who are brokers approached me to capitalize a brokerage firm. My brothers tried to persuade me with this argument: Let's get on the other side of the table—own the casino so to speak—so we'll make money whether the customer wins or loses. I decided it would be better to own the casino than be the one sitting slumped at a slot machine with a bucket of nickels, so I capitalized a large brokerage firm in Dallas.

I continued to actively trade full time. I bought and sold just like the textbooks said using the so-called "conventional wisdom" and employing the methods I learned at very expensive seminars. I made money at times but I lost a whole lot too.

Most important, I never felt comfortable with what I was doing. I watched CNBC, *Market Watch, Moneyline,* and every financial show I could tune into. I read trading books, newsletters, and stock charts until I was blurry-eyed. I felt like a deer caught in the high beams of an eighteen-wheeler. I kept trying to figure out why most people lose money trading while the big boys on Wall Street just keep on chalking up their profits.

Then a phenomenon occurred while I owned that firm that changed everything in the world of stock trading—the Internet.

As recently as the late 1980s, the information superhighway was not available to individual investors. Instead, we relied on reading the business sections buried in *Newsweek* or other weekly magazines. There was really no reason to keep more abreast than that because, in the 1980s and the decades before, the market went up only 10 or 15 points on a good day; on a bad day, it went down 10 or 15 points. Back then, it was usually a slow steady climb all day or a slow steady drop all day.

But with the sudden availability of the Internet to millions of people in the 1990s, any individual with a PC had access to a superhighway of instant "real-time" financial news and information and the added maneuverability of trading online at the slightest whim.

Early in this new era, a new breed of individual investors known as day-traders started to emerge. These individuals fed on the constant stream of information to make several trades a day; sometimes, several trades an hour. Initially, many were successful. They were like jet skiers zooming around a cruise ship (the old-school market makers), and day-traders were making a lot of money without many waves.

Then the media started to shine a light on these unusual blurry-eyed trading creatures who seemed to sweat caffeine and feed intravenously off multiple computer screens. When the word got out about the success of the early day-traders, the rush was on. It seemed everyone and his brother started day-trading. The vast influx of individual traders jumping on the online trading bandwagon fed by instant information available on the Internet was one of the contributing factors that led to the volatility of the market today.

Unlike a few years earlier, when the market would typically go up or down only 10 to 15 points a day, just the Dow can now jump up or down hundreds of points every day. It doesn't much matter if there's a negative or positive opening because the market can go up and down up to 50 times a day.

Toward the end of my involvement with the brokerage firm (and before the late 1990s bubble/bull market), the market was so volatile that 85 percent of my customers were losing money. We would have 30 people a month who lost so much money that they would drop out of the market. They would be replaced with 30 more "innocents." It was a revolving door of customers and I hated it. It seemed unethical to bring customers on board knowing that the vast majority of them were going to lose money while we profited from the commission on their trades.

I became increasingly frustrated and finally overwhelmed watching people investing their hard-earned money in the stock market only to lose their savings that was meant for their retirement. But at the time I wasn't sure how I could better serve these investors.

Then a year before I left my brokerage company, a computer programmer who was a customer came into the office. He had designed an investment program for a major brokerage firm. His program used summation formulas and algorithms.

His computer program was really just a numbers game. Though very interested in its capacity, I saw lots of inconsistencies and erroneous summation formulas plugged into it. I suggested some changes that could better the program, but those changes were rejected.

But I wanted to do far better for individual investors, especially those I saw being devastated in the marketplace. I also envisioned making this tool accessible to investors directly so they could benefit without going through a broker. The broker already had the advantage. I wanted to "take care of the customer."

I started developing my own summation formulas and algorithms using 50 technical indicators (there are literally hundreds of them but each one has its strengths and weaknesses so I selected only the best). Over the next few years, I spent hundreds of thousands of dollars building a successful trading platform. I hired the best and the brightest software engineers in the country to take incredibly complex algorithms and create a simple but effective program that would help people make money investing in the stock market.

Eventually, we chose seven key data factors for two summation formulas to determine the buying and selling dynamics for every stock. (I will be more specific about these formulas in the next chapters.)

Like the computerized programs used by the big boys on Wall Street, I applied hard unemotional information about supply, demand, volume, and numerous algorithmic indicators to create an intricate mathematical formula that could be applied to any stock, any time, in any market. To keep up with the big boys, it was vital that the program run thousands of simultaneous calculations applying a precise mathematical formula to help investors take emotion out of the investing process. This technical, computerized approach is known as "program trading" and it operates at a level that no human brain can process. (Program trading is explored much more in the next chapters.)

Technology leveled the playing field for individual investors, but it was intimidating when it first became available because it was too complex and overwhelming. I realized that I needed a simple way for individuals to easily understand the output of the complex calculation technology. I decided to use red and green lights to signal entry and exit opportunities, and Wizetrade™ was born.

Now I'm fulfilling my mission to take care of the customer. Again, you don't need Wizetrade™ to be successful, but its charts in this book will help me show you what works—and why—in the wonderful and sometimes wild world of investing in stocks. I promise this insight will serve you well.

Thanks for the advice, Dad.

BUYERS AND SELLERS/SUPPLY AND DEMAND

What is the most influential reason for a stock's value to go up or down? It is the number of stocks being bought versus the number being sold.

The value of a stock rises and falls based on the amount of demand for it. When the demand for a stock is high, buyers bid higher prices to entice sellers to sell it to them. Conversely, when demand is low, sellers have to lower their prices to attract willing buyers.

The simple dynamic of supply and demand—buyers versus sellers—is the most important reason a stock's price goes up or down. Here is the bottom line:

- If there are more buyers than sellers, a stock's price goes up.
- If there are more sellers than buyers, a stock's price goes down.

Plain and simple.

Like any market, the stock market depends on buying and selling inventory. Its inventory is stocks.

The simple matter of buyers versus sellers (supply versus demand) has been a constant since the beginning of mankind when one cavemen indicated "I want what you have" and another one responded "How *much* do you want it?"

But how do you track the buyers and sellers to your advantage?

PROGRAM TRADING

Have you ever felt that the big boys on Wall Street knew something you didn't? That there was a secret to what works on Wall Street and what doesn't? That a simple method exists that instantly tells them when to buy or sell a stock regardless of how the rest of the market is performing?

I'm going to break the code of silence and let you in on the secret here. In short, I'll show you how they take the guesswork out of trading. There really is a secret to trading on Wall Street—a secret used by big institutions and Wall Street brokerage firms every day. It's called *program trading*. Major institutional investors know that to be really successful trading stocks, you must be completely programmed at a level no human brain can process.

How did the big boys solve the problem? They program their computers to make the decisions for them. They use hard *unemotional* information about supply, demand, volume, and numerous algorithmic indicators to come up with an intricate mathematical formula that can be applied to any stock, at any time, in any market. Then they let their computers run thousands of simultaneous calculations to buy or sell stocks. They literally take the emotion out of buying and selling and base their trading decisions on number-crunching formulas. Every day, big institutions let their computers buy, sell, and trade based on what their programs are saying.

Computers triggered the stock market crash in 1987 when computerized programs all said "sell" at the same time. The big boys got out and left all the little investors like you and me holding the bag. To avoid another crash like this, regulators placed trading curbs on institutions that force them to turn off their program trading software once the market moves too fast in one direction. However, regulators didn't curb individual investors like you and me because they never thought we would have access to this type of sophisticated software. Fortunately, times have changed. Technology has leveled the playing field and access to these software programs has allowed us all to reap the rewards.

Why then do some Wall Street firms do better than others when making trading decisions? The reason is because a computerized program is only as good as the data that's fed into it and the formula each firm has developed to crunch its numbers. Different firms choose different criteria depending on their theories on what moves the market. Because many firms depend on what I strongly consider to be misleading figures (e.g., fundamental analysis, PE ratios, or superfluous technical data), I contend that you can do better than the vast majority of "experts" if you focus on the most reliable criteria for stock analysis.

TECHNICAL ANALYSIS

Let's make a distinction between *technical analysis* and *fundamental analysis* up front, and let me state that I am a strong proponent of technical analysis.

Fundamental analysis relies on sales, earnings, and growth. No doubt you have heard horror stories about companies that report great sales, earnings, and growth, yet the price of their stock still goes down. Could it have something to do it with the public's distrust that the fundamentals are absolutely accurate because these figures are reported by the companies?

Technical analysis is a method of evaluating stocks by relying on indisputable market data such as price, volume, and buying and selling interest. The price of a stock is subject to the market pressures of supply and demand—the bottom line for technical analysts to buy, hold, or sell. Technical analysis has been used by major institutions and top Wall Street analysts for years as a key indicator of when to buy and sell stocks. Using technical analysis keeps you from letting your emotions rule how you invest your hard-earned money. Wizetrade™ utilizes carefully chosen technical analysis criteria.

The psychology of the investing crowd constantly seesaws between emotions of fear and overconfidence. In a volatile market, panic overrides during the bad times while greed is foremost during the good. The charts of a technical analysis program reflect this wavering psychology and the flow of cash in and out of each stock. Fundamental analysis disregards this psychology because it is based only on sales, earnings, and growth whether investors are actually buying or selling a company's stocks.

In the past couple of years, more and more individuals have taken advantage of the benefits of investing based upon technical analysis. The advances in technology have allowed the software and investment industry the ability to create software programs that are easy to learn and use, effectively taking the guesswork out of investing.

When used according to the rules, technical analysis can become the best thing to ever happen to your financial future.

Can Individual Traders Master Technical Analysis?

To be successful, individual investors need a technical analysis program that is easy to use so, in a short amount of time, they can understand and confidently use it effectively to increase their potential net worth.

Wizetrade™ was created to present technical analysis in a simplified charting system, incorporating green and red light indicators much like the ones you find at street intersections. This system takes into account seven critical data factors to determine point of entry, point of exit, and trend analysis.

For the record, here is how Wizetrade™ works.

- Wizetrade™ begins by gathering the first four of the seven critical data factors—the open, high, low, and close of each of eight time intervals. (These eight time intervals are different for each trading strategy, ranging from long term to day trading. Three time intervals that are constants are month, week, and day; the five remaining shorter-term increments differ with trading strategies.)
- Then it compiles the next two of the seven critical data factors—the up tick and down tick for each of the eight time intervals.
- Then it gets the last, and most important, of the seven critical data factors—the historic data, which is exponentially weighted to volume because of the intrinsic price properties relating to the stock's price performance.
- Wizetrade™ then takes these seven critical data factors and integrates them into two proprietary summation formulas—the X + Y (represented

by the green lines and lights) and the X − Y (represented by the red lines and lights).

- Both summation formulas are then calculated by an algorithm, which is then displayed by either a red or green light indicator.

I realize that for most of you this mumbo jumbo tech talk starts to sound like the trumpeting "bwah bwah bwah" of the adults in a Peanuts cartoon. Yet the red light/green light indicators in Wizetrade™ could not be any simpler to interpret. Does the average investor really care about all of the details of the algorithms that go into arriving at these simple indicators? No. Investors should be aware that the program is sound in logic and assessment, but what really matters is that the program actually works and is simple enough to understand and use.

The Wizetrade™ algorithms work for any type of trader. Whether the trader is looking at holding a position for months, weeks, days, or minutes, the exact same key indicators are used.

The long-term/monthly chart in Figure 7.1 is a classic example of the accuracy and simplicity of the Wizetrade™ system. (In the following figures, the red lines in Wizetrade™ charts appear as black lines, and the green lines appear as gray.)

In the chart in Figure 7.1, Wizetrade™'s trend of ImClone reflects two trading opportunities for the long-term investor (in this case, long-term refers to months, not years).

- In March of 2001, a buy signal was given at $31.63. The sell signal was given in June 2001 at $54.30.
- Another buy signal occurred in July 2001 at $42.61, and with the sell signal in December 2001 at $71.98.

The per-share profit on these two trades equates to $52.04. If the individual trader bought as few as 100 shares, the profit equates to $5,204 or a 70 percent return on just two trades. The investor had a signal to get out of ImClone before it fell sharply, thus avoiding the loss felt by other investors who held on to it during its major drop.

At it's height in November 2001 (as of this writing), ImClone stock was worth $75.45 per share. Based on Wizetrade™'s technical analysis, there was a long-term signal to sell ImClone (the red/sellers line overtook the green/buyers line). If someone had ImClone stock in their retirement account in Novem-

FIGURE 7.1 *Sample Wizetrade™ Chart*

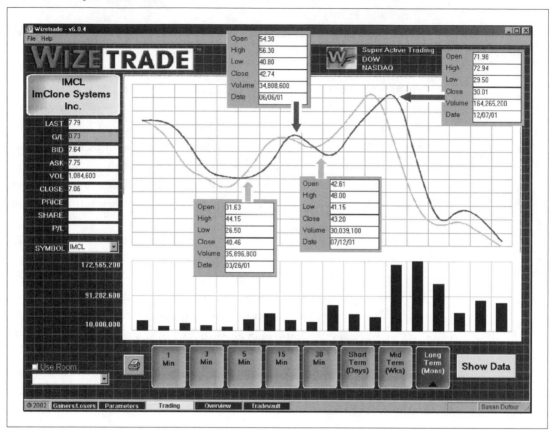

ber 2001, they could have protected their nest egg by utilizing Wizetrade™'s indicators and getting out of the stock, keeping roughly $67 per share more than what they would have gotten for it six months later in May 2002.

Here's a thought: The latest data shows that individual investors make up 39 percent of the market. If the majority of these investors were able to master the art of technical analysis and not let their emotions rule them, we may see a more stable market.

ENTRY AND EXIT SIGNALS

For simplicity, there are three visual factors to easily identify entry and exit signals, as shown in the ImClone chart in Figure 7.1:

1. A *fresh cross* of red and green lines within one time frame (each vertical line on the chart equals one time frame)
2. A *good angle* of momentum (between 12:00 and 2:00 on a clock face for going long and between 4:00 and 6:00 for going short)
3. A *strong separation* representing stability between the buying and selling pressure

These three factors are simple to identify and understand and you can quickly adopt this type of technical analysis.

There will be much more about these factors—called FAST™ (using initials from **f**resh cross, good **a**ngle, **s**trong separation, and the **t**iming of entering and exiting trades)—in the next chapter.

CHARTING THE COURSE

Let's compare to a typical technical analysis chart used by the pros (shown in Figure 7.2) to the Wizetrade™ chart (shown in Figure 7.3).

The daily Wal-Mart chart in Figure 7.2 reflects some very important and useful data. However, how simple is it for the average investor to successfully interpret this complex chart? Do you want to take the time to learn how to interpret this complex presentation of information?

Now, compare that chart to the one in Figure 7.3. This chart is the Wizetrade™ daily chart of Wal-Mart. It contains a lot of the same complex information of the previous charting system, yet the presentation of this data is laid out in a very simple format. It now becomes a matter of looking for the three visual factors used to identify the entry and exit points—fresh cross, good angle, and strong separation. Simple and accurate.

BASIC FOUNDATION FOR RECOGNIZING TRADES

It doesn't work to urge people to think outside the box without giving them the tools to climb out.

LAURIE DENNAVANT, 3M Health Care Systems

Until now, choosing stocks has been a complex, time-consuming task that, at best, was still a guessing game for the vast majority of individual investors.

FIGURE 7.2 *Typical Technical Analysis Chart for Wal-Mart Stores*

Courtesy of StockCharts.com

Today, if you're empowered with comprehensible tools to conduct real-time stock analysis instantly, then you can pick the best of the best as well as anyone else out there as long as you know what to look for.

We have already established the great dynamic that drives a stock up or down: buyers and sellers, supply and demand. We also determined that program trading (using computerized systems) is the way to go because it provides you with tools to conduct unemotional stock analysis and can compute thousands of calculations simultaneously beyond the capability of any human mind. It is the edge that's needed by traders in today's fast-moving markets.

FIGURE 7.3 *Wizetrade™ Chart for Wal-Mart Stores*

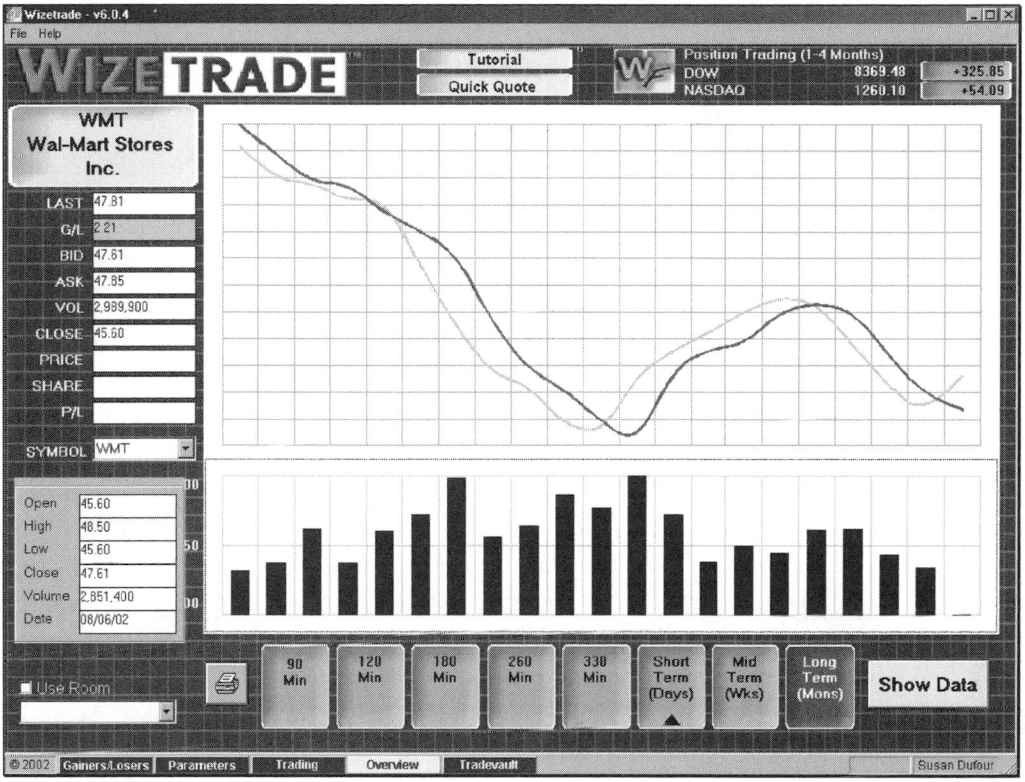

First Things First

What good is a technical analysis system if the average investor can't comprehend and confidently use it to make choices about buying and selling stocks to increase their net worth? An investor's objective is to make trading choices simply, quickly, and reliably. You need to be able to instantly analyze stocks and confidently choose trades without being "paralyzed" by analysis.

An important capability provided by Wizetrade™ is the ability to quickly evaluate and recognize whether a stock is a good trade or not. In Figures 7.1 and 7.3, you saw illustrations of how ImClone and Wal-Mart were evaluated with Wizetrade™'s simplified system.

Regardless of what system you use, you need to be able to quickly check the status not only of stocks in your current portfolio but also ones you're interested in or just curious about. It is also imperative that you never enter into a trade without having an exit plan that covers every possible outcome when that stock inevitably fluctuates. Only then will you have the peace of mind that comes with having a plan.

The Three Wizemen™

With Wizetrade™ trend recognition software, your stock decision-making process becomes as simple as "red light-green light." Stop or Go? If there is more buying pressure during a current time interval, the light is green. If there is more selling pressure during a current time interval, the light is red.

The first filtering system for a potential investment is to have the three indicators for long term (the current month), mid-term (the current week), and short term (the current day) all moving in the *same* direction. In Wizetrade™ vernacular, these three indicators (month, week, and day) are "in agreement" when all three are green or red—comprising the three Wizemen™.

If all three Wizemen™ are green, you might consider going long. In this case, long does not refer to trading long term but to buying a stock for any amount of time with the intention of making money as it increases in value—as it gets longer, if you will. If all three Wizemen™ are red, you might consider another kind of trade called shorting. I know shorting is a new concept to almost all of you so there will be much more about shorting in Chapter 10.

Notice that in both cases I said "might consider"; again, these Wizemen™ indicators are your first filtering system, not your last. (Again note that the red lines appear as black, and the green lines as gray.)

In the Wizetrade™ trading screen in Figure 7.4, we can literally see in seconds that the stocks for Verity (VRTY), Cablevision Systems Corp. (CVC), and Knight-Ridder (KRI) all have the three Wizemen™ in agreement—the month, week, and day indicators are all green. Quickly, you can recognize three possible long trades. The stock for Pep Boys–Manny Moe (PBY) is a candidate for a short trade.

The stock for Enzon, Inc. (ENZN) is giving mixed signals because the Wizemen™ are not in agreement (one green light and two red lights) and should be avoided for now. If the month, week, and day are not all the same color, the three Wizemen™ are not in agreement.

The more trends you have in agreement, specifically the long, mid, and short term, generally speaking, the more conservative the trade is. Why? When the indicators on each of these trends indicate the same movement, it will take a larger movement in the opposite direction to reverse that trend.

FIGURE 7.4 *Sample Wizetrade™ Trading Screen*

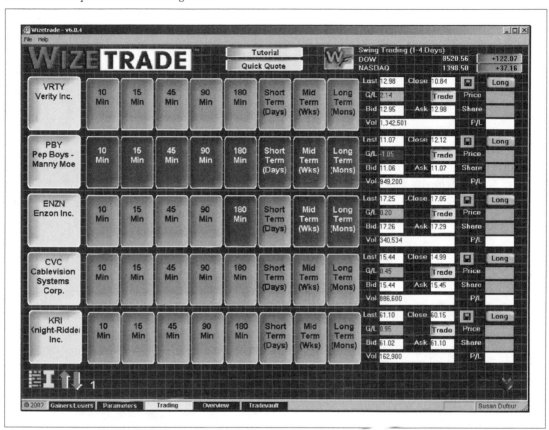

The long term (month) is the strongest and most important indicator in trend recognition. Why? The long-term trend is a broader perspective of the buying and selling pressure on any stock. On any given day, you may have more buying pressure than selling pressure. Stocks vacillate back and forth all the time. Some days they're up and some days they're down. What you need to do is get a collective or broader view of all of these days combined to see what the investing masses are really up to.

Think of the month as the foundation of your house. You wouldn't build your house on a weak foundation. A month curve that does not show strong separation and strong angle of momentum is weak. Building on this type of foundation—when the month is weak—is risky. Pass on it. There are better fish in the sea.

Trading Screen

The trading screen, like the one in Figure 7.4, gives you the ability not only to look at the series of lights in eight time frames, but also to glimpse at the most current price and the trading volume of a stock for the current trading day. This screen gives you an overview of the direction in eight time frames for any stock you choose. In fact, you can view five stocks at a time on one screen. The constantly updated Dow and Nasdaq ticker can be found in the upper right-hand corner of all Wizetrade™ screens.

Figure 7.5 takes a quick gander at the information provided for each stock on the right-hand side of the screen. Again, this is not to toot Wizetrade™'s horn but to indicate to you the important up-to-the-second factors that you need at your disposal when trading.

1. The last price at which the stock trades
2. The gain or loss from the previous trading session
3. The stock's bid and ask prices
4. The stock price at the end of the previous trading session
5. The stock's trading volume thus far for the current trading day
6. The price at which you purchased the stock and the number of shares, which allow you to track "real" trades or "paper" ones
7. The color-coded real-time profit or loss of the trade (after deducting execution costs)

Price per Share

At first glance, the current price of a stock is irrelevant to determining whether a stock is a good trade or not. The price alone does not indicate whether a stock is a bargain or overpriced. After all, a $50 stock may be a great buy while a $20 stock may prove to be a stinker, or vice versa; it depends on the particular stock. That being said, it is imperative that you have up-to-the-second quotes on bid and ask prices.

Taking nothing else into consideration, set your sights on stock prices within a range that fits your own budget and trading strategy. If your trading budget is limited, you may find lower-priced stocks to be more attractive because you can buy more shares and diversify by buying shares in several different companies. For example, if your total trading budget is $5,000, then stocks costing $100 per share are probably too high for you because you can

FIGURE 7.5 *Sample Stock Data Provided on Wizetrade™'s Trading Screen*

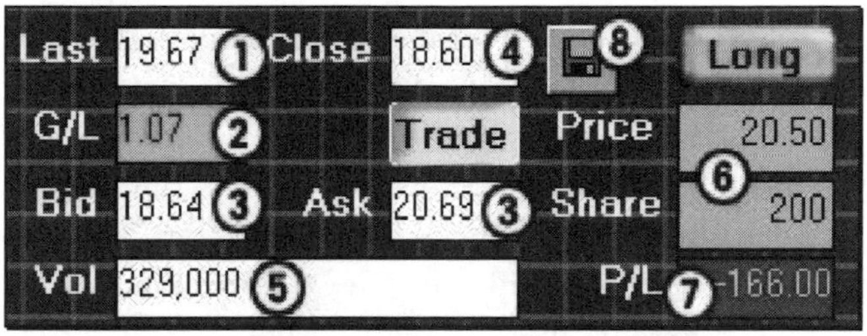

only buy 50 shares in that range and you don't want to put all your eggs in one basket by buying 50 shares of only one company. By choosing various stocks with share prices that average $20 apiece, you can buy 250 shares with that same $5,000 budget. (When budgeting, don't forget those pesky broker commission fees that you'll be paying for trades.)

However, some traders don't feel comfortable trading stocks that are low priced (for example, those costing under $10). Again, it's up to you and your risk tolerance. That's why Wizetrade™ offers other parameters from which to choose and various criteria to consider, which we'll get to shortly.

Obviously, when you're ready to buy or sell, you're only interested in the most current prices being quoted—not what was quoted in yesterday's paper. The two prices you need are:

1. *Bid price.* The highest price at which someone is willing to buy a stock.
2. *Ask price.* The lowest price at which someone is willing to sell a stock.

The difference between the bid and ask prices is called the spread. For example, if the bid price is $15.00 and the ask price is $15.05, the spread is 5 cents. The bid price is always lower than the ask price (hopefully only by pennies) so there is a profit margin for the market makers to make it worth their while to be the middlemen for trades. If the spread is too high, then the stock may be volatile and deserves further exploration (e.g., spiking volume indicates unusual trading activity and often influences higher spreads until the stock settles down).

If you want to *buy* a stock, look at the *ask* price because that's how much it will cost you to buy the stock. If you want to *sell*, look at the *bid* price because that's how much other traders are willing pay you for your stock.

FAST™ (But Not Furious)

Be careful about the lure of green lights. They may prove to be weak or flat upon closer inspection. They should, however, be used as an encouraging first filter to investigate further when all three indicators (the three Wizemen™) are in agreement. Before making a trading decision, you need to identify that the movement is new, strong, and stable. To clarify this, we go to other charts.

For simplicity and quick recognition, Wizetrade™ provides three visual factors you can easily identify when looking for entry and exit signals, as is evident in the ImClone chart presented in Figure 7.1: fresh cross, strong angle, and strong separation (FAST™). Figure 7.6 highlights these three factors.

The *fresh cross* (1 in Figure 7.6) is when the green (solid) and red (dashed) lines first cross each other during the most pertinent time interval for your trading strategy. Entering a long trade, you look for the green line freshly crossing over the red one.

The fresh cross signals the beginning of a new trend. Why is it so important to enter a *new* trend? Simple: You want to ride the trend for as long as possible by recognizing it at the onset, therefore increasing your profits. If you invest two or three time periods *after* the fresh cross occurred, you might still make money—but not as much as the investor who jumped in and rode the wave when the fresh cross began. (You want to make as much money as possible here, don't you?)

An "embryonic cross" in which the lines have crossed but haven't really established a trend, and yet signals that it's too early to determine if the trend will hold. Wait and see.

The *good angle* (2 in Figure 7.6) is represented by the angle of the green line. When looking to go long, look for the green line to be on top of the red, pointing upward between 12:00 and 2:00 on a clock face. A good angle confirms heavy buying pressure versus heavy selling pressure.

FIGURE 7.6 *The Three Factors of FAST™*

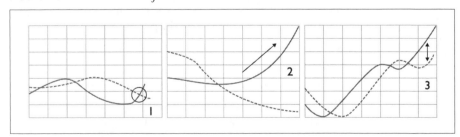

Proper separation (3 in Figure 7.6) is represented by recognizable white space between the green and red lines, confirming the stability of the trade. It also confirms that the separation between the buying and selling pressure is significant enough to remain strong for a while.

If the green and red lines are close or converging (not separating as we'd like), it is still a *potential* bounce situation (a bounce is when converging lines separate once again and is as good as a cross), but if you try to anticipate a bounce or a cross, you might as well anticipate a loss. Be patient and wait for the buyer or seller momentum to choose sides. If you jump into a stock with an "I hope it works out" attitude, you're in the wrong stock.

If a stock is moving sideways (when both the buying and selling are flat, resulting in no separation) and you still enter into this trade, you've just put your money on hold and out of your hands. It's better to use your trading money elsewhere. Look for stronger signals.

Whether the trader is looking to hold a position for months, weeks, days, or minutes, the same key indicators of the three Wizemen™ and FAST™ are used. If you trade against the system, then you are at your own risk.

Ideally, you find a "freight train" when all three Wizemen™ indicators make you exclaim "Wow!" A freight train is a stock that has maximum strength and momentum where the month, week, and day *all* have increasing angle, separation, and momentum. The freight train analogy for trading long strongly implies that the trend can't be easily stopped because major buying momentum is in play (in the case of shorting, the selling momentum is very prominent).

The "T" in FAST™ stands for *timing*—when exactly to enter and exit a trade. Timing is totally dependent on your trading strategy (for example, you enter a trade with a far different mind-set if you are monitoring it all day long as opposed to if you're going on a month-long cruise and have no access to a computer during that time).

The following trading strategies are fully addressed in Chapter 8, but here's a quick glance:

- *Position/intermediate trader.* One who enters a trade intending to hold the stock for several weeks or a few months at a time.
- *Swing trader.* One who enters a trade intending to hold the stock for one to five days.
- *Active trader.* One who enters a trade intending to hold the stock for no longer than one day.

Trends as Friends

A lot of stocks have repetitive trend patterns. (Remember our ImClone example in Figure 7.1, moving up and down like a roller coaster, offering three buy and sell opportunities before it hit the skids?) For example, Company XYZ's stock might have a recognizable trend about every three weeks in which a fresh cross occurs every three weeks or so and it repeats itself again and again. This is more common than you might think.

If history repeats itself that consistently for a particular stock, you might be successful trading with that cyclical trend. Of course, you also want as many other factors in play as possible to guide you so you don't get burned on a hunch based solely on past performance. But don't ignore the trend. The trend can be your friend. It can be so predictable that it can be like shooting fish in a barrel.

All green lights turn red sometime just like a traffic signal. If you're driving along a road and you see a green light a mile away and it's still green a half-mile away, expect it to turn red as you get closer (*all* green lights turn red eventually unless they're malfunctioning). Once the traffic light turns green again (a fresh cross), you should be assured that you can make it through the intersection because you saw how long the light stayed green as you approached it. That's an example of a trend in your favor. Green light/red light. Sound familiar?

When money flows *out* of the market for either one day or much longer periods like a bear market, it is very difficult for a stock to rise in value. Yes, it happens but it's less likely. This is what's called "swimming against the tide." When this occurs, you have three options, listed from first preference to last:

1. Go with the market trend.
2. Take a cash position (stay out of a trade).
3. Go against the trend on a short-term basis (the highest risk of the three).

Volume

Trading volume is very important to bear in mind when inspecting a stock. For one thing, you don't want to get stuck with a large number of shares of a stock and then find that you can't exit with a decent price whenever you'd like because the stock isn't trading enough and therefore lacks liquidity. Lower volume also often has a greater spread between the bid and ask prices which puts more money into the market maker's hands, not yours.

If a stock has good movement (a green line going up at a perfect angle with great separation between the lines), look at the volume. If the volume is consistent, you know that the movement of the stock is sound and can be sustained. On the other hand, if the volume is unusually high—as with a volume spike—you know that the price or momentum has been skewed. Most likely, the momentum cannot be sustained and the stock will fall back to its previous movement. When trading, always keep an eye on the volume and make sure you're not riding a sudden and erratic wave of buying or selling that is often quickly followed by a return to the status quo or a crash of the wave.

Trading volume reflects the current supply and demand for that stock. Here are some good volume guidelines when going long.

- Consistency is the key.
- 400,000 shares *average* daily volume (over the course of the past ten trading days) is a good minimum that makes it easier to enter and exit trades with smaller spreads, good liquidity, and good flow of your order with your broker.
- Even though volume is figured into Wizetrade™'s summation formula and algorithms, volume bars shown on the charts help you to visually inspect consistency and watch for spikes (unusual volume traded).
- Stocks with steady but increasing volume, good liquidity, and strong signals are always your best and safest bets.

The chart in Figure 7.7 shows a stock exhibiting steady but increasing volume that meets good trading criteria.

There is a reason we place a heavy emphasis on volume. You may hear on the news that the market is down 100 points that day on *huge* volume. This is bad because it will take huge buying volume to reverse. If the market is down 100 points on *light* volume, it is far less significant because it will take a lot less volume as a counterbalance to return those 100 points. A big movement on little volume suggests some people or a few institutions felt compelled to pay more for the stock then they had to.

FYI: In Wizetrade™, in order for a trend light to change colors while the volume remains somewhat consistent, it takes the opposite (buying or selling)

FIGURE 7.7 *Sample Chart of Good Trading Volume*

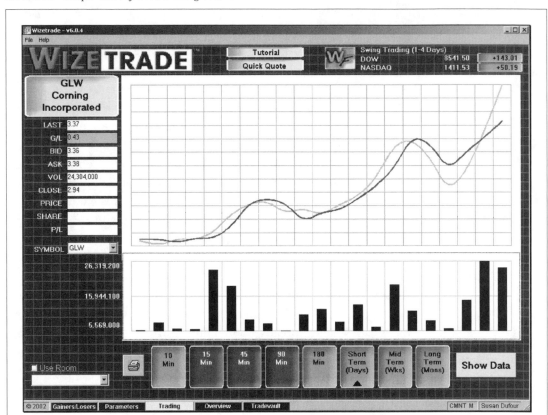

pressure to be in control for approximately one-half of that time frame, if the volume remains consistent, to reverse the trend.

Every stock has a typical daily volume of buying and selling, but a major movement can be recognized as a spike in the volume for that day. Be careful of stocks that are *one-day wonders*. An example would be a stock that usually averages low volume, say 20,000 shares per day for weeks, but all of the sudden trades 800,000 shares one day. If the volume drops back the next day, it is a possible sign that active traders herded in and out and then moved on to the next hot stock.

Instead, stocks with steady but increasing volume, good liquidity, and strong signals are usually your best and safest bet.

When stocks go up, you want to see strong volume heading to the upside. This indicates that strong bids to buy (most likely fueled by institutions) are pushing them up. As much as we all like to think that we influence the markets, inevitably, it is institutional trading that really influences the direction of the markets. Thus, unless we're ready to buck the system on riskier trading strategies, we need to try to trade "with the stream."

Often stocks cycle up on strong volume and pull back on thin volume. Keep in mind that stocks are always going to correct downward after a strong cycle. However, if the correctional cycle is influenced by thinner volume than what moved your position up, you're more likely get another move in your favor.

CONCLUSION

You might find it interesting that brokers, analysts, and institutional investors struggle at first with Wizetrade™ because they have ingrained conceptions of what they are supposed to utilize when making stock choices. They muddy it up with their old ways of stock analysis—even though Wizetrade™ is built on the most basic concept that buyers and sellers determine the market.

The folks who have the easiest time with these concepts and those most quickly successful with Wizetrade™ are those who have never directly traded on the market before.

As the opening quotation says, "It is also crucial to unlearn old knowledge that has outlived its relevance." If you're a "newbie," count yourself lucky that you don't have to unlearn as much as the pros in this new world of investing.

It's time now to get personal by identifying your trading strategy, practicing it until you're comfortable, and then going for it to make some bucks trading.

8

LET'S GET PERSONAL

Applying Foundations to
Your Trading Strategy

Management by objective works—if you know the objectives.

PETER F. DRUCKER

Let's start with an old Wall Street joke.

What do you call a losing trade?
A long-term investment.

Then there's the old adage that you should *always* invest in stocks for the long term, regardless of fluctuations in the market. The reason for this is that historically over the course of the past century, the stock market as a whole has consistently grown 11 to 12 percent per year. This is true, but what we're focusing on here is investing in individual stocks, not in the market as a whole.

Many experts advocate this buy-and-hold investment strategy of holding onto stocks through thick and thin. But in today's volatile market when major indexes like the Dow and Nasdaq swing up or down as much as 5 percent in a day, I think this passive investment strategy should now be more aptly named buy-hold-and-pray. How many folks during a bear market are simply sitting on all of their losses, praying for a rebound? Millions. If they would trade more actively with a plan (including entry *and* exit strategies), they would know to sell whatever stocks reached the exit point they predetermined *before* entering the trade.

The concept of long-term investments should have changed with the advent of the information age and the ensuing vast influx of individual investors into the market. Long term used to be 10 to 30 years; today, I contend that it's about 6 months, if that long. In the past, stock movement was like watching paint dry; now it's month to month, if not day to day. There also used to be lifetime loyalty to a company's stock, but misguided loyalty only confuses the issue and can keep you in a bad investment far longer than you should.

The Spanish Armada used to be the most powerful force on earth. It was finally defeated by small boats using the guerilla tactics of hit and run. Using this analogy, the buy-and-hold strategy of our grandparents is like the Spanish Armada. Today's strategy is more hit-and-run with this volatile market. Again, long-term investing used to mean years; now it's months.

"WHERE'S MY NICHE?"

In the previous chapter, I introduced three trading strategies:

1. The *position/intermediate trader* enters a trade intending to hold the stock for several weeks or a few months at a time.
2. The *swing trader* enters a trade intending to hold the stock for one to five days.
3. The day-trader enters a trade intending to hold the stock for no longer than one day.

It's up to you to identify your trading style and strategy, especially taking into account your risk tolerance and the amount of time you want (or do not want) to dedicate to investing.

If you have a full-time day job and cannot be at the computer to monitor stocks all day, you would be a position/intermediate trader. If you're able to sit at the computer all day, you may have the time to be a swing or day-trader if you're so inclined.

Obviously, the shorter the trade period, the closer you need to monitor the trade to identify your entry and exit points. Therefore, swing trading and day-trading require more time and focus on stock movements than position trading. Is that what you want to do (or have time to do)?

You should also take into account your time zone. The market in New York City is open from 9:30 AM to 4:30 PM. If you live in the Pacific time zone, that's 6:30 AM to 1:30 PM. Because most fresh crosses occur during the first hour of trading, as a swing trader or especially as a day-trader, you had better be an early bird or a very late bird to monitor the market while on the West Coast. If you don't, you'll miss out on the trading opportunities of those two strategies. Position traders are concerned with week-to-week or perhaps day-to-day movements, not hour-to-hour movements, so they can sleep late.

When you need the money is another factor. How long are you comfortable tying up your investment dollars? How quickly do you need to realize profits (hopefully)? Months, weeks, one day? If you know what you want, you're in a far better position to figure out how to get it.

How much time do you want to spend on investing? How active do you want to be in managing your money? If you're not sure, choose a trading strategy and practice it by *paper trading* (not making real trades but practicing the methods for whatever strategy you want to explore). While practicing, you may find that swing or day-trading is not to your liking or is too demanding of your time, or that position trading isn't as hands-on or exhilarating as you'd like it to be. You can then choose a different role and play again until you find your niche. While you're pretending you lose no money and can establish your game plan.

What is your risk tolerance? This subject has been covered several times in this book, but when choosing specific stocks, always evaluate the risk before entering a trade and have an exit strategy to get out.

The more trends you have in agreement, specifically the long, mid, and short term, generally speaking, the more conservative the trade is. Why? When the indicators on each of the trends are all in agreement, it would take a larger movement in the opposite direction to reverse that trend. But if you are willing to take more risks in hopes of higher rewards, you may choose to ignore the long-term trend and trade on a shorter-term basis, simply taking advantage of the day-by-day or even minute-by-minute fluctuations in the buying and selling pressures in play.

By knowing your risk tolerance level, you will know which trends you want to confirm in agreement. If you really enjoy the excitement of day-trading, like to be at your computer all day long, and have the time to keep a close eye on shorter trends, you may find that the reward ratio of trading off the minute lights is perfectly suited for you. That doesn't mean that every day-trader will disregard the agreement of long-, mid-, and short-term trends (that we have come to know as the three Wizemen™). Some will and some won't. Those investors who disregard trends in agreement have a higher risk tolerance than those that don't.

Now let's get more specific about risks involved for each trading strategy. Keep in mind that the biggest risk may be not taking enough risk, meaning not investing enough in stocks.

TRADING AND TRIGGER WINDOWS

The basic principles and criteria of the three Wizemen™ and FAST™ apply for all three trading strategies. If you want to be on the conservative side (not straying from the trends), explore candidates only if the three Wizemen™ (the month, week, and day) are in agreement—that is, they're the same color, looking for all green lights for going long. Also observe the FAST™ criteria—a fresh cross or bounce in the "trigger" window, a strong angle of momentum, and a wide separation between the lines.

"But where do I look if I'm a position trader instead of a day-trader?"

The three main trading strategies we've been looking at in this book—position, swing, and day-trading—have different trigger windows. The trigger window, which is immediately to the left of the trading window, is very important because it is where the trader identifies and times his or her good entry and exit points for making trades. It is critical to have a fresh cross in the trigger window (with strength and stability for longer terms).

Trading Strategy	Trading Window	Trigger Window
Intermediate Position (weeks or months)	Week	Day
Swing (days)	Day	180 minutes
Day (same day)	180 minutes	Minutes (10, 30, 60, or 180)

Always start on the month to determine the foundation for trades, and then proceed to the week and day. For whatever trading strategy that suits you, concentrate on its trading window for entry points and the trigger window for exit points.

POINTS OF EXIT FOR *ALL* TRADING STRATEGIES

For exit points, you look for a strong movement of the red line to overtake the green line in your trigger window. At the point when the red line does cross over, the chart's lights will turn red. The lights in the shorter-term time frames to the left of the trigger window will give you a heads-up that the takeover is possibly imminent and you should pay close attention.

If the trigger window chart reflects a weak upward or flat movement by the green line, you might choose to hang on a while longer until a better signal develops. You don't want to jump out prematurely if the green line has the potential to become more dominant again by bouncing up and away from the red line and separating as they resume going upward. Pay close attention until the trend continues or reverses itself and then make your trading decision. (To determine your selling/exit point, you should look for the same FAST™ signals as when you bought the stock, only now look for the red line overtaking the green line for a fresh cross, angle of separation, and divergence.)

When the stock price goes against you, sell it back to avoid further losses. You should set an absolute maximum loss you're willing to sustain. Identify that exit point and stick to it.

Figure 8.1 is an example of an exit point for an intermediate position trade, so we're looking at the day window for the trigger point for an exit signal. (I won't show exit charts for all three strategies because they all look similar, but remember that the trigger window is different for each strategy.)

For this stock (F5 Networks Inc.), we are looking at the day/short-term chart because that's the trigger point for this intermediate position trade. We see a strong movement by the sellers (the red line) overtaking the buyers (the green line) on the far right-hand side of the screen. Because there is also a strong angle of momentum and proper separation of the lines, we know it's strong movement by the sellers and decide to get out.

Here are a couple notes about the chart screens I'm using for illustrations in this chapter:

- The month, week, and day charts go back 20 time periods with the most current on the far right of the graph.
- The minute charts go back 50 time periods, again with the most current on the far right of the graph.

FIGURE 8.1 *Example of a Position Trade Exit Point*

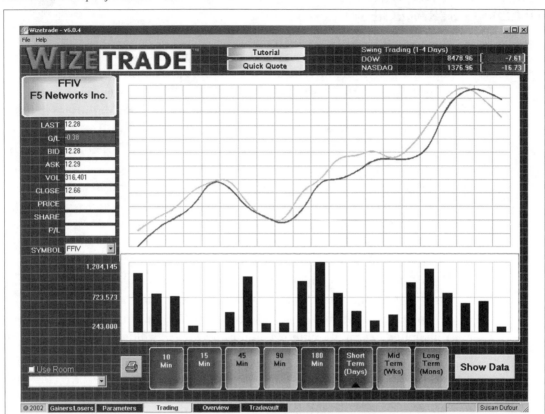

In all cases, the most current lines change as the stock's movement changes with buying and selling pressures (they're "moving windows"); everything to the left is "fixed" because it reflects the history of the preceding time periods.

The volume bars at the bottom of the screen indicate relative movement (i.e., momentum) over the 20 to 50 time periods.

Now let's explore the three trading strategies in more depth.

THE THREE TRADING STRATEGIES

Intermediate Position Trader

The intermediate position trader enters a trade intending to hold the stock for several weeks or a few months at a time.

If you have a full-time day job conflicting with market hours (9:30 AM to 4:30 PM Eastern time), then you may consider adopting this strategy. Position trading is also a good strategy for those who don't want to (or cannot) monitor their computer throughout the day, or at least during the first hour and last hour of the market because those are the most active trading periods. The position trader is concerned with week-to-week and day-to-day movements, not hour-to-hour or minute-to-minute movements.

Relatively speaking, the position trader is more conservative than a swing trader or day-trader because he or she invariably looks for *all* trends to be in agreement, namely the current time frames for long (month), mid (week), and short (day) all going in the same direction. The position trader wants to see more buying than selling momentum for trading long during each of these three time frames to meet the three Wizemen™ criteria. The position trader also tends to look for the FAST™ criteria to be in full effect.

Entry Criteria for Intermediate Position Traders

Entry Point (trading window)	Week/mid-term with a fresh cross of the green line, angle of momentum, and proper separation between the lines (FAST™)
Other Wizemen™ Windows	Day/short term and month/long term crosses are fresh or may be running a little longer
Average Volume over the Last Ten Trading Days	400,000 or more

The chart in Figure 8.2 displays Yahoo! stock that meets these criteria for entering an intermediate position trade. (Note that we're looking at the week/mid-term chart because that's our trading window as an entry point for a position trade.)

An intermediate position trader should be consistent with the type of trading strategy he or she has chosen. For example, be patient when the minute and hour time periods fluctuate up and down. As a rule, ignore them or you'll enter or, more likely, exit a trade too soon.

But, what if you are a position trader with more risk tolerance? If you stray from the more conservative trends, practice it (paper trade) until you reach a confidence level to trade with real money. For example:

- You might trade on a cross in your trading window from last week instead of a fresh one during the current week (but because you likely missed one week of taking profits, I'd look for a different trade to enter).

FIGURE 8.2 *Example of a Good Position Trade Stock*

- During a bull market, you might consider a stock in which the month has a buying momentum for an indefinite period (several months) instead of a relatively fresh cross.

Exit point (trigger window) for intermediate position traders. Look for the day / short term with a fresh cross of the red line with angle of momentum, proper separation between the lines, and significant volume supporting the new strong selling momentum.

As a position trader, you can basically ignore the smaller minute windows turning red unless you see a wave of red coming your way toward the day / short-term position. Then you might perk up and pay attention because an exit point might be imminent.

Also be aware that as a position trader possibly holding a stock for months at a time, it's possible you'll be holding stocks during quarterly earnings announcements. These are required to be reported by companies (every three months). Pay attention to (or better yet, anticipate) those announcements relating to the stocks you're holding because there's often a significant swing up or down depending on the news.

Swing Trader

The swing trader enters a trade intending to hold a stock for one to five days.

Large institutions trade in volumes too large to move in and out of stocks in such a short period due to regulations. This leaves the one-to-five day time frame for the individual to trade a "swing" stock with less competition from large institutions than one might otherwise encounter.

It is possible for folks with full-time day jobs (or who have other daytime conflicts) to swing trade but it's important that they monitor their trades on the computer during the first hour and last hour of the market because those are the most active trading periods.

I believe that beginning traders can quickly learn how to swing trade. Swing trading offers potential profit-making benefits for position traders if they're willing to change gears and learn this strategy by practicing it. A swing trader gets relatively quick feedback and might feel more motivated and disciplined over the course of a few days compared to waiting the weeks or months required of a position trader. Which one fits your style and discipline? (In contrast, day-trading may prove too great a white-knuckle ride for you because it requires constant diligence in monitoring stocks minute to minute if not second to second.)

Different swing traders have different risk tolerances. Some are more conservative and like to trade stocks only when the three Wizemen™ and FAST™ are in agreement. Others are willing to take a little more risk and may go against the long-term or mid-term trends. How much risk are you willing to take in hopes of a greater reward?

Let's look at the entry criteria for a more "conservative" swing trader.

Entry Criteria for "Conservative" Swing Traders

Entry Point (trading window)	Day/short term with a fresh cross of the green line, angle of momentum, and proper separation between the lines (FAST™)
Other Wizemen™ Windows	Week/mid-term and month/long-term crosses are fresh or may be running a little longer
Average Volume over the Last Ten Trading Days	400,000 or more

The chart in Figure 8.3 displays Abercrombie & Fitch Co. stock that meets these relatively conservative criteria for entering a swing trade. (Note that we're looking at the day/short term because that's our trading window as an entry point for a swing trade.)

FIGURE 8.3 *Example of a Good Swing Trade Stock*

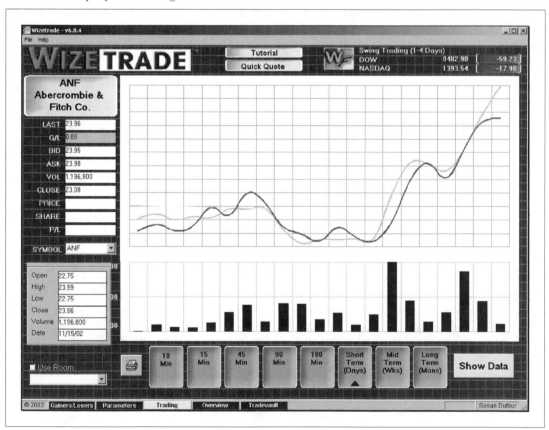

What options do you have if you have more risk tolerance as a swing trader? (If you stray from the more conservative trends, practice it—paper trade—until you reach a confidence level to trade with real money.) For example:

- You can lower the average volume criteria (though I would never go below 300,000 average volume for a swing trade over the last ten trading days—you need liquidity to sell it back).
- You might trade on a cross in your trading window from two days ago instead of a fresh one during the current day (but because you likely missed one day of taking profits, I'd look for a different trade to enter).
- Find stocks where the mid-term and long-term indicators are in agreement and the short-term indicator is the opposite color and is *close* to making a cross or bounce and put them on your "radar screen" for when the day/short-term indicator *does* cross or bounce.
- Even riskier, you can ignore the long-term when the short-term and mid-term indicators are in agreement.

Exit point (trigger window) for swing traders. Look for the 180 minutes or shorter period with a fresh cross of the red line with angle of momentum, proper separation between the lines, and significant volume supporting the new strong selling momentum.

Active Trader

The active trader enters a trade intending to hold the stock for no longer than one day and does not hold the position overnight.

It is really impossible for folks with full-time day jobs (or other daytime conflicts) to day-trade because of the constant monitoring necessary for this strategy. But if their schedule permits a day or two to day-trade (as opposed to trading every day), then they might day-trade part time.

Unlike my encouragement for you to explore swing trading, I can't be as enthusiastic for active trading unless you're willing to be very diligent and disciplined. Remember that I once financed a firm in the late 1990s and saw many people lose their shirts active trading. Though I fully believe in Wizetrade™ as a great resource for active trading, almost every unbiased investment expert will tell you that active trading requires some degree of luck and requires extreme discipline for you to remain focused every hour, minute, and, in some circumstances, every second of the trading day.

One must also be willing to accept losses along with gains.

Different active traders have different risk tolerances. Some are more conservative and like to trade stocks only when the three Wizemen™ and FAST™ are in agreement. Others are willing to take a lot more risk and go against the long- or mid-term trends. Regardless, active trading is by far the most risky of the three strategies I'm presenting to you.

Let's look at the entry criteria for the most "conservative" day-trader.

Entry Criteria for "Conservative" Active Traders

Entry Point (trading window)	180 minutes (or far smaller time frames) with a fresh cross of the green line, angle of momentum, and proper separation between the lines (FAST™)
Other Wizemen™ Windows	Day/short-term, week/mid-term and month/long-term crosses are fresh or may be running a little longer
Average Volume over the Last Ten Trading Days	600,000 or more

The chart in Figure 8.4 displays Sapient Corporation stock that meets these relatively conservative criteria for entering a day-trade. (Note that we're looking at the three-minute chart as our trading window for our entry point for this day-trade.)

What options do you have if you have more risk tolerance as an active trader? (Again, if you stray from the more conservative trends, practice it—paper trade—until you reach a confidence level to trade with real money.) For example:

- You might trade on a fresh cross in your trading window minutes ago instead of during the current period (but because you likely missed one period of taking profits, I'd look for a different trade to enter).
- You might consider trading one-day wonders where the day/short term meets the FAST™ criteria but ignores the mid-term and long-term indicators.
- Even riskier, you can ignore the long-term where the short-term and mid-term indicators are in agreement.

FIGURE 8.4 *Example of a Good Day-Trade Stock*

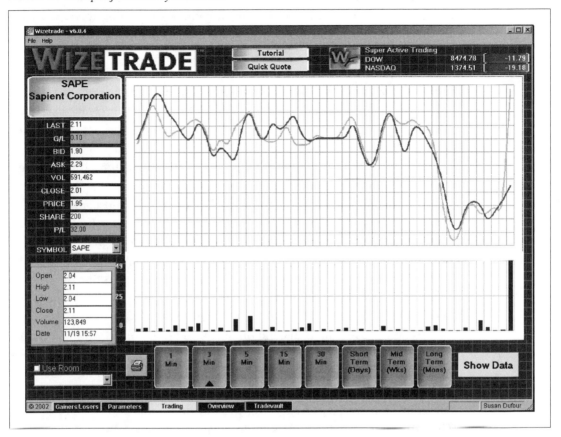

Active traders should pay attention to the markets by paying attention to the Dow and Nasdaq movements. Most active traders know that most of the intraday movement occurs in the first hour and last hour of trading.

Active traders must decide exactly what their plan of attack is and strictly adhere to it. They have short periods of time that they are dealing with and little room for error. They should not flip-flop back and forth, doing one thing sometimes and doing the opposite other times. Active traders need to find their groove on what minute lights off of which they like to trade and stick with it.

Exit point (trigger window) for active traders. Based on the minute chart you choose for your entry, look for and use a consistent, smaller time frame chart with a fresh cross of the red line with angle of momentum, wide separation between the lines, and significant volume supporting the new strong selling momentum.

A couple more cautionary thoughts for potential active traders. If you intend to day-trade, you *must* select a computerized system which provides real-time (up-to-the-second) price quotes and one which provides extremely reliable data on buying/selling momentum as well as volume activity for each individual stock you want to day-trade. (Wizetrade™ provides all of this information, but regardless of where you get this vital information, it must be extremely quick and accurate to be useful to a day-trader.)

Also, you should choose a brokerage that executes and confirms trades extremely quickly; better yet, if you're day-trading, choose a brokerage that provides *direct* access to Wall Street trading firms to buy or sell at a specific price almost instantaneously. (Direct-access trading commissions tend to be lower; however, commission costs are still high for day-traders due to the huge numbers of trades that day-traders tend to make, even if they negotiate a discounted price of $5 to $10 per trade for high activity.)

Because active traders depend on making a few pennies or dimes on each extremely short-term trading transaction, they often need to trade very high volumes to make their trades worthwhile. For instance, if a active trader buys 1,000 shares costing $25 each—or $25,000 total—and the stock goes up 10 cents per share during the short term of the day-trade, that's only a $100 profit. Therefore, many active traders trade on margin—buying stocks from their broker with borrowed money to increase their buying capabilities. Remember that trading on margin means you borrow money. No matter how short the time of the loan, you have to not only pay back your loan but also interest *and* commission for the trade. If the stock dives when trading on margin, you can go into a hole quick.

Considering all I've said about active trading, is that what you want to do? There are high possibilities of reward in day-trading accompanied by higher risks.

INTRADAY STOCK MOVEMENTS

Position traders should not be overly concerned with minute-to-minute trade movements on the stock market. However, for swing traders and day-traders, there are three important intraday stock movements on Wall Street of which they must be aware:

1. Most fresh crossovers occur in the first 30 minutes to 60 minutes of the market's open.
2. The market is often flat during midday (sometimes referred to as midday consolidation). Why? One reason is the market makers eat lunch then!
3. Activity often accelerates during the last hour of the trading day.

I will explore intraday stock movements more in the Chapter 9, but you should be aware that the first and last hours of the trading day (Eastern time) are traditionally the most active periods, so shorter-term traders need to be most alert during those two time periods.

CONCLUSION

You can always change your strategy or technique if you're in a positive trade and your signal strengthens dramatically—stay with it.

However, in the same vein, if the trade goes against you, cut your losses—sell it. Don't change your strategy in an attempt to salvage the trade in the hope that it will change course. Be disciplined but don't ignore very strong or very weak signals telling you what you should do. If you trade on mixed signals, you get mixed results. Timing, patience, and consistency are the keys to success.

9

TIPS AND PITFALLS

It's not whether you're right or wrong that's important, but how much money you make when you're right and how much you lose when you're wrong.

GEORGE SOROS, Soros Fund Management

PAPER TRADING

A tourist in New York City asks a passerby, "How do I get to Carnegie Hall?" The passerby replies, "Practice, practice, practice."

How do you become comfortable and proficient with a new trading strategy before investing real money? Paper trading, paper trading, paper trading.

In the previous chapter, I introduced the three main trading strategies— position, swing, and day—along with trends to look for in each one plus entry and exit points. I also suggested ways that you can stray a bit from these strategies if your risk tolerance is greater than the conservative trends.

By this point, you might already identify with one strategy over the others due to your circumstances, risk tolerance, and time available to devote to trading. If so, that's great. However, if you have never invested on your own before *or* if you are a seasoned trader who's embarking on a new strategy, I implore you to paper trade—to practice before using real money—until you grasp the concepts and get the criteria and trading signals that work for you on a consistent basis down pat.

By paper trading first, you can save thousands of dollars while honing your skills until you're consistently getting positive results and feeling comfortable with your success rate. If you try to learn while investing real money, you might find yourself out on a limb that is being sawed off behind you.

If you're a newbie, learning any new trading program or strategy is like learning a foreign language, no matter how easy it may be to understand.

Experienced traders need to take even *more* time to hone a new system and strategy if they've depended on analyses that may no longer apply to their new path. For example, excellent drivers from America have to learn to drive on the left side of the road if they move to England. American drivers and experienced traders have many ingrained notions that may not apply to their new situation and can be not only distracting but disastrous.

It is important to enter a paper trade as if it's real. For example, only paper trade with dollar amounts that you actually have available to trade. Even though you're practicing with pretend money, be realistic. If you paper trade with $100,000 but you actually have only $5,000, then you might have fun pretending with the exaggerated amount but you won't learn anything pertinent to your real-life situation. Paper trade with your real-life budget.

Track your trade by keeping a journal, or using a spreadsheet like Excel or Lotus 1-2-3, or simply writing it all down on a pad of paper. Wizetrade™ includes a Tradevault screen (shown in Figure 9.1) that easily tracks all of the necessary criteria for paper and real trading and it provides a real-time account of your position.

What information should you track in order to learn while paper trading? When entering a paper trade, it is important to track the following:

- The company name and symbol
- Date
- Entering price (the ask price)
- Number of shares you're "buying"
- The fee to your broker to enter the trade
- The reasons you identified this stock as a good trade to enter

To calculate entrance and exit fees, assume that you're trading online without your broker's advice (which costs more) because you're making the

FIGURE 9.1 *Sample Tradevault Screen*

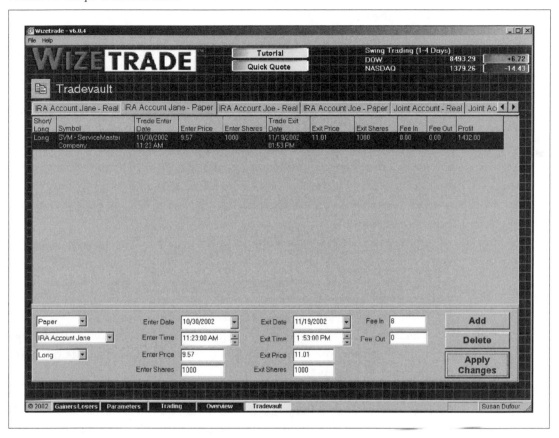

trade on your own. Use a low fee of $8 or $9 for both entering and exiting the trade.

When exiting a paper trade, track the following:

- Date
- Exiting price (the bid price)
- Number of shares you're selling
- The fee to your broker to exit the trade
- The reasons you're exiting the trade

To do the math simply multiply the entry price by the number of shares (or the exit price by the number of shares), minus the fees to get into (or out of) the trade. You can then determine if you would you have made or lost money on the trade.

In your evaluation, pay special attention to the reasons you entered or exited each trade. Then look back at the stock's charts to see if you could have pinpointed a better entry or exit point by paying more attention to trends and curves or ignoring misleading ones. Did you enter the trade too soon or too late? Did you exit too soon or too late? In hindsight, should you have not entered the trade at all? In other words, ask yourself if you could have done better.

By paper trading and learning from your experience prior to real trading, you test your proficiency in whatever strategy you've chosen and you can build your confidence in a short period of time. Paper trading also will alert you to any deficiencies in your trading strategy that need further exploration and experimentation.

I'm often asked how many times to paper trade before moving on to real money. It depends. I know, you want a definite number but it really depends on the individual and the strategy. The goal is to hit your stride by earning confidence and a success rate with which you're comfortable. If you can do that after five paper trades, wow. If it takes 60 or more, so be it.

The most common mistakes that newbies make are not trading a fresh cross for their trader type, not keeping a log of their paper trades for self-evaluation or not paper trading at all.

Once you test and prove your methodology and consistency by paper trading, you can start trading real money. I suggest you start real trading with relatively small lots and continue to ramp up as you become successful. For example, you might start your real trading with 100 shares and then ramp up to 200, 300, 400, and so on, as you gain confidence.

If you move on to real trading and want to begin exploring another strategy, paper trade *again* with the new strategy, no matter how similar it may be to the one you've learned, until you reach a level of success with which you're comfortable.

Learn to Eliminate Emotions While Paper Trading

While paper trading, people have a tendency not to let emotions influence their decisions to enter or exit trades because real money isn't involved. However, emotions are far more likely to enter the equation when you begin trading with real money because the prospects of gaining or losing become real, not imagined.

The main emotions involved in trading are fear and greed. Emotions come into play more when you are *exiting* a trade than entering one—and probably not in ways you might expect. What's fascinating is that you would expect fear to influence a trader to bow *out* at the first sign of trouble; instead, it influences the trader to stay *in* losing trades too long because he or she fears losing even more money and hopes that somehow, some way, stocks will climb back up. Humans have a built-in antidote to fear, which is hope, and hope can wreak havoc on our investment choices. I've seen too many investors that knew they owned bad stocks but held them hoping the market would reverse and push the prices higher. Mistake. The market isn't moved by hopes.

Greed also impacts an investor's actions negatively, but not in the way you might expect. Greed influences a trader to get *out* of a successful trade too soon because there is an overwhelming temptation to cash in his profits prematurely while the stock is still trending upward.

The important thing to remember is that if fear/false hope or greed prevails, you will lose money. But if you establish a successful exit strategy while paper trading when emotions are *not* involved, and trust that experience when making the transition to real trades, you will not fall prey to the pitfalls of your emotions.

You can test the emotional impact on trading by "playing like" you're using real money when paper trading. Make a few trades based on your gut feelings, not your analysis of the criteria, and see how greed and fear tend to rear their ugly heads to influence bad decisions. By experiencing these emotions during paper trading, you'll also learn to recognize these feelings should they creep up during real trading. You'll then be reminded of the importance of sticking to your strategy.

Intuition and gut feelings can be valuable in many areas of life, especially in making many personal decisions, but they're not at all reliable when applied to investments. (Remember the adage, anticipate a cross then anticipate a loss?) If you were successful paper trading without emotions, don't change your plan when you start using real money by trading on hunches or anticipating events that haven't happened.

If you ignore all the signals and indicators of your trading strategy, it's like running through 100 red traffic lights with a devil-may-care attitude. You may make it through a few unscathed, but the numbers will catch up with you.

How you think or feel a stock will perform is irrelevant. As boring as it sounds, be mechanical and disciplined when investing. This sounds simple, but it's difficult to ignore our instincts and gut feelings. If you must exercise your emotions, gamble on hunches in Las Vegas; trade on trends on Wall Street.

INTRADAY STOCK MOVEMENTS

Stocks go through several market cycles and phenomena daily. Also they don't go up or down in a straight line; they go through many "steps" or "movements" throughout their trend.

If you have established a strategy for entering and exiting trades as a position or swing trader, be disciplined and don't second-guess yourself while stocks fluctuate throughout the day as they invariably will do. The right time to trade is based completely on an individual's trading objectives. However, regardless of your strategy, it is important to understand that most trading activity typically occurs during the first and last hours of the trading day.

Buying Stocks at the Close

Most fresh crossovers occur during the opening hour of stock markets, driven largely by institutional buyers and day-traders. For this reason, you might find it advantageous to closely watch for the following scenario at the end of the day: If a stock on the Wizetrade™ trading screen has a red day but a green week and green month with good separation on the curves, you might watch to see if the minute lights start to turn green and the lines start to cross and move to the upside near market close. If this occurs, it could potentially move much higher in the morning. By buying this stock at the close, you could potentially catch a fresh cross early the next morning that could continue moving strongly to the upside for several days. (This does contradict the "anticipate a cross, anticipate a loss" rule, but if the minute lights support the trend in that direction, then it's up to you to make the trading decision based on your trading strategy.)

Midday Consolidation

In a midday consolidation pattern, there is strong movement in a stock during the morning, a period of consolidation or downturn around the middle of the day, then a resumption of momentum in the afternoon. However, the midday flatness or a slight dip may simply reflect that market makers are eating lunch! My advice to position and swing traders: Be patient during midday (Eastern time).

Price Spikes

Price spikes are quick but strong temporary moves in stock prices either up or down. The market makers may be "playing around" with the stock. Pay attention but don't panic, especially if you're a position trader; you don't want to sell a stock that's experiencing a temporary movement.

In case you haven't noticed, I'm not a big fan of brokers and market makers. Because they control the premarket and postmarket activity, they can play games with your hard-earned money by creating temporary "false" spikes hoping to suck you into stocks on gap ups and scare you out of stocks with gap downs. That's why I developed the red light/green light program. By utilizing the principles of Wizetrade™ for evaluating the week and day with a strong month, you can avoid the pitfalls that most people make when they're unduly shaken out of their position while these Wall Street games play out.

An example of a price spike is the *Nasdaq suck down*. This drop in stock price typically occurs when a stock is in a great uptrend, but perhaps is now three to four weeks into that trend and starting to get a little tired. For example, stock is at $20 per share, up $2 for the day. It has great curves but the trend started when the stock was at $12 per share, so it's already gone up 80 percent at this point. In this case, the market makers may artificially move the price down—a temporary price change that should only affect day-traders. However, sometimes this move startles longer-term traders. Position and swing traders should check to see if the stock was moving up strong in the morning. If it drops down hard in the afternoon but the month indicator shows the stock in a great uptrend with the week early in its cycle (with a fresh cross), the position or swing trader may find this to be an opportunity to buy even more, not to bail out prematurely during the "suck down."

This is called the Nasdaq suck down because it generally happens with Nasdaq-listed stocks since Nasdaq allows after-market activity during which the market makers' games might go unnoticed (the NYSE does not have after-market trading). Although a suck down can also occur sometimes with NYSE and other listed stocks, it occurs with greater regularity among Amex/Nasdaq/OTC stocks.

Gap Down at the Open

Although the scenario could look solid—a stock's trend moving higher and showing more buyers than sellers, the week trendline looking fairly fresh, and a solid month—sometimes the market as a whole goes down at the open taking a stock with it.

If the stock gaps down but an uptrend is in place (the month and week curves are excellent), keep inspecting the day chart. If it remains separated, the stock will fill in the gap all day.

A *bad gap down,* however, is when the stock gaps down at the open but the short-term minute curves look wrong. Check the news and information on that stock because it is a probable indication that something materially negative has happened with that company. This is not just a morning gap down, but a complete reversal in sentiment.

If a swing cycle is extended, a gap down may mean the end of a cycle at which time the stock becomes more volatile. The green line on the day starts to arc over and converge hard to the right—becoming unstable on a short-term basis. However, as long as the long term is rock solid (FAST™ in month, week, and day), the minute lights may not be indicative of how the stock will move on a long-term basis.

TRADING ON EARNINGS ANNOUNCEMENTS

A publicly traded company is required by law to publish its earnings reports four times a year (once each quarter). "Earning season" lasts about three weeks during the months *after* each quarter ends, that is, in January, April, July, and October. Therefore, there are 12 weeks (three weeks per quarter) in which to be aware of the earning season.

Why are these important times for the investor to remain alert? Stocks rise and fall when investors react to whether the company exceeds target expectations or fails to do so. In fact, stocks rise and fall in *anticipation* of the earnings reports if rumors are being floated or if analysts on TV or major investment Web sites make predictions. I have poo-pooed trading on analysts' predictions on TV, but if they name sources to back up their predictions on good, bad, or neutral earnings announcements, then check the charts. They may give you a heads-up to major buying or selling movement even before the announcement is actually made.

Much like the release of blockbuster movies which are staggered throughout the busy viewing periods so they don't all open at once, these earnings reports are made in bunches over the course of the three weeks. I've noticed that the analogy can be carried further: If a company has an especially positive earnings report, it'll look for less competition on a release date and go out of its way to generate "buzz" so everyone notices it (much like with the way studios release movies with Oscar potential on special days in late December). If a company is a dog with disappointing news, then it might try to slip the report in on a busy day or at a less newsworthy time of day so fewer people will notice the "bad reviews." However, blue chip stocks on the Dow will be noticed whether they have good, bad, or indifferent announcements.

Most of these announcements are made right after the market closes or right before it opens; a few, however, are made during trading hours.

I have implored you not to trade on your *own* emotions or gut reactions, but don't ignore the behavior of the *masses* because they are likely to move a stock up or down based on euphoria or hysteria during earnings season. While disciplined traders don't trade on their own emotions, they should be cognizant of the major reaction the masses cause when they emotionally support or reject a company (out of fear or greed) when earnings announcements are released. Carefully watch movements on the charts and let them be your guide because they reflect real—not perceived—buying and selling movement.

Specialty Trade during Earnings Season

This specialty trade works for active traders if the earnings announcement is scheduled just before or after the market closes (remember that *anticipation* of the news—if widespread—can have as great an effect on a stock's movement as the actual announcement). Consider the following:

- Arrange lights to super active trading style—1, 3, 5, 15, 30 minute lights.
- One hour before the market closes, there may be a two to ten point move in the stock.
- Go in and out of the position in the last hour of trading. Don't hold the position overnight.
- Pay special attention to Nasdaq stocks that trade after hours when earnings announcements are often made, making them more volatile during these quarterly periods.

ALLOCATE

No matter how short term your trading strategy is, you can still *allocate* by never putting all of the money you've set aside for stock investments into one company—putting all your eggs in one basket so to speak. (I'm making a distinction here between the money you allocate for stocks and that allocated for other investments such as in bonds, real estate, insurance policies, cash, etc. When I refer to 100 percent of your investment in this chapter, I'm only referring to money you've allocated for *stocks*—not *all* of your investment money.)

If a company in which you've invested all your money suddenly and inexplicably goes down the drain, you've lost everything. Think of what happened to Enron recently when many employees had no choice but to have all their funds tied up in their company's stock—they lost the entire value of their retirement savings.

No matter how safe an investment opportunity seems, don't ever put more than a small fraction of your assets into one company. It just isn't worth the angst.

Here is a simple allocation model for stocks that you can easily replicate (this is not a plan of action, just an example).

If you own stocks in ten different companies with an equal amount of money invested in each one, then each stock represents 10 percent (out of 100 percent) of the money you've set aside for stocks. If nine of the ten stocks break even (neither going up or down) but one goes bankrupt, you lose 10 percent of your investment. However, if you put a stop limit order of 10 percent on each stock (meaning you've instructed your broker to sell any stock dropping 10 percent below the level at which you bought it), nine of the stocks will be unaffected because their price remained the same; the one that heads south is stopped and automatically sold after losing 10 percent as you directed. Now, you've only lost 10 percent of one stock. In other words, you've lost the value of one-tenth of 10 percent of your stocks—or 1 percent of your total investments.

See how that works? Allocating your stock investment money among ten stocks lowers your risk of big losses. While there's no such thing as a risk-free investment, there are ways of getting around the highest risks. Like I've said before, the more risk you're willing to take, the more likely you are to have a large return, or, on the flip side, the loss of all of your investment capital.

There's a saying that has more than a grain of truth in it: There are old traders and bold traders, but no old bold traders.

DON'T HOLD ON TO LOSERS

It's quite common for people to sell their winners prematurely and hold on to their losers for too long, hoping they'll improve in the future. If a stock is not performing up to your expectations (and reaches the threshold of your predetermined exit strategy), get rid of it and put the money elsewhere. In the same vein, when you make an investment mistake, rectify it by selling it and moving on (comfort yourself with the fact that you are far from alone). Learn from your experience, move on, and don't dwell on it again.

INSIDER BUYING AND SELLING

Buy When Insiders Buy

If those who run and oversee a company are buying their own stock, chances are that they think the value of the stock will rise. Because they are in the know—aware of hundreds of details about the company's operation and future prospects that those of us on the outside could never hope to know—follow their lead if you can. How can you do that? Simple. Insiders must disclose to the SEC all trades in their own company's stocks and those transactions are immediately available to the public in the SEC's EDGAR database online. If you see an upward trend in the stock in which you're interested, check EDGAR to see if the bigwigs are buying. For example, insiders may know about a new product that's about to be introduced that will increase revenue substantially, so they invest in their own company with their own money. That activity is not only legal (as long as it's properly reported), it is a great indicator to outsiders like us.

Sell (Run Like the Wind!) When Insiders Sell

While it's obvious now in hindsight, if investors would have checked SEC's EDGAR database during late 2001, they would have seen Enron executives like Kenneth Lay and Jeffrey Skilling selling hundreds of thousands (cumulatively millions) of shares of their own company's stock. *Not* a good sign. They obviously weren't selling that much stock to buy a swimming pool or put their kids through private schools—they were bailing out.

The charts gave you clear signals to sell Enron stock at about $78 per share. These shares now sell for about $1 apiece. You *could* have confirmed these failing signals by checking EDGAR. Why the SEC didn't notice the red flags months before the scandal, I don't know. Perhaps it is because this agency is extremely understaffed and underfunded. The point is *you* could have discovered it before the stock dropped precipitously by making a few clicks in EDGAR to see what Enron corporate executives were doing with their own company's stock. That information was available to the public *before* the scandal dominated the headlines.

TWO MYTHS

Mutual Funds

Myth: Mutual funds have smart managers. They will give you diversification and will protect you.

Three-quarters of all managed mutual funds *underperform* the stock market's average return. That's 75 percent! How "smart" can these managers be? Also, if you evaluate all the individual stocks in the vast majority of mutual fund offerings in charts like those Wizetrade™ provides, you'd find obvious losers in the fund's "family." Why buy any package with losers built into the trade? Of course, we all want diversification in our portfolio, but nobody's definition of diversification implies a mix of winners and losers.

In additional to this, mutual fund managers of load funds charge 3 to 8 percent up front as a sales fee. They justify this up-front load fee by not charging administrative fees later on.

If you have the wherewithal to be independent with the know-how to evaluate stocks and a computerized program with all the real-time data you need, why invest in a package of stocks not of your choosing? You can do far better on your own by choosing all of our own stocks. If for some reason you want to diversify your stock portfolio with a package deal, then I urge you to invest in *index funds* which, at a very low cost, track a segment of the market's returns, which invariably outperform mutual funds.

Mutual fund managers actively select which stocks to purchase. Remember that managers are human and were no less immune than individual investors to the seduction of dot-com companies during the recent boom years. Many loaded their funds with these flashy stocks and when the bubble burst so did the value of most mutual funds.

Index funds are immune to seduction. They don't change with whims or gut feelings. The index fund manager sets up the portfolio to mirror a market index. Examples of these funds include the S&P 500 stock index (often called Spiders, stock symbol SPY), the Dow Diamonds (DIA), or the Nasdaq 100 general technology fund (QQQ), though there are over 100 index funds available.

Beyond using index funds as an investment option, you can also track different sectors by plugging in the stock symbol of an index fund into a program like Wizetrade™ to gain insight into how that part of the market is performing. For example, if you checked out QQQ (sometimes called the Qs), you'd instantly get a snapshot of how the Nasdaq 100 general technology fund is doing overall by checking its month, week, and day trends just like you would with an individual stock. If the QQQ index is doing well and trending up, you might consider buying that index fund *or* you might dig a little deeper within that index to find a particular stock to buy—looking for the best of the best, of course.

PE Ratios

Myth: The PE ratio is the most important indicator of the value of a stock.

No doubt you have heard of the PE ratio because, second only to the price of a stock, it is a number often cited in the media. PE ratio is the price of the stock (P) divided by its earnings (E) per share. A stock with a PE of ten or higher is often touted by brokers and analysts as a hold-or-sell candidate because the stock is considered overpriced, while a PE under ten is touted as a buy because it is underpriced. Wall Street dangled this benchmark and the media took the baton and ran with it without question.

Accountants know that investors look at a PE ratio as a vital indicator, so that's why they monkey around with earnings reports. If the earnings are manipulated (often legally) or fabricated (as we've seen far too often in this age of Enron and WorldCom), then the equation as a whole is based on misinformation or an outright lie and therefore cannot be trusted.

Yet the media reports PE ratios as if they're the holy grail for predicting future stock returns. When media analysts report a PE ratio as the reason to buy or sell a stock, don't shoot the messengers, just ignore them.

'TIS THE SEASON

For those of you who have been in the investing game for a while, you might have noticed that stock investments tend to perform better during the winter months than in the summer. (I'm not sure why exactly; maybe it's summer doldrums or the fact that market makers and institutional investors on vacation.) I was astonished to find how great the discrepancy was when I came across facts quoted in Yale Hirsch's 2002 edition of *Stock Trader's Almanac.* Mr. Hirsch tracked the S&P 500 since 1950. If you invested $10,000 in the S&P 500 in 1950, by mid-2001, these would be your results:

- From May 1 to October 31, the $10,000 would have grown to only $11,408
- From November 1 to April 30, the $10,000 would have grown to $314,056

Now, don't let this scare you out of the market for six months out of the year. After all, he tracked an index of 500 stocks. An individual stock can perform well during down markets or poorly during up markets. That's why I feel strongly about choosing your own individual stocks rather than a package of funds.

FLY ME AWAY

I always wanted to learn to fly. Yet I didn't want to devote years to obtaining and maintaining a pilot's license. Then I would see these flying contraptions at boat shows called ultralights. They are basically powered paragliders that promised "the magic of simple, elemental, pure flight." I gave one a try at a one-day flight class and was hooked. I bought an ultralight and now I fly with the wind in my face and an unobstructed view of the countryside 100 feet below.

You can only fly ultralights in winds of up to 15 mph, so I only fly early in the morning or just before nightfall because where I live there are wind thermals during the day which produce increased wind speeds. My trainer told me there would be days when after 30 minutes of preparation the wind would pick up just before I'd be ready to take off. According to my trainer, if the wind speed is borderline there will be times when I'd be tempted to fly anyway. Then he told me something I will never forget: "It's better to be on the ground wishing you were in the air than being in the air wishing you were on the ground."

Later it occurred to me that this advice was valuable for trading as well. Both flying and trading have inherent risks that can be minimized if you set parameters and stick to them. You've got to trust the indicators and then have the discipline to take action or not, depending on what the indicators tell you.

Never force a trade. You can't force money out of the market. Let the trade come to you. There are windows of opportunity. If you miss one, let it go. Patience and timing are the keys to successful investing.

And remember, if it's not a good day for flying or for trading, there's always another day.

10

ADVANCED STRATEGY
Short Orders

All things are difficult before they are easy.

THOMAS FULLER

Several times in this book, I have referred to shorting a stock, going short, or simply used the word *short* and said I'd explain it later. Well the time has come.

What does shorting mean?

Shorting is when you sell a stock before you buy it. If you think the stock is going down in price, you sell it at the higher price and then buy it back at a lower price.

This is where you might respond, "Whoa, Nellie. How the heck do I make money doing that? By shorting, I sell a stock *before* I buy it? And after selling a stock that I don't even own, I root for it to drop in value, and *then* I buy it back for a profit?" Absolutely. This trading technique is used very successfully every day by many individuals and institutions. In the midst of a bear market, it is a strategy that should be considered.

Once you understand the concept and how and why it works, executing a shorting trade is easy—*if* you have the right tools for recognizing good shorting opportunities *and* understand what you're doing. Short selling is just one technique you can add to your trading toolbox, if it matches your risk tolerance and investing style. (Having read this book, you already have all the basic terms at your disposal, so you don't need to learn a new vocabulary in order to short.)

Many savvy investors, however, can't wrap their minds around the concept of shorting because it doesn't seem natural to trade on stocks that are going down—it's like having to adjust to running red lights instead of stopping. To add to this, a person who goes short must *borrow* the stock from an institution (namely in the form of a margin loan from a brokerage for the cost of the stock) and pay interest for the duration of that loan. This is the price of being allowed to sit at the table to play the shorting game and it applies to every short investor, even those as rich as Bill Gates.

Scared off yet? I hope not. Give me another chance to explain it. But remember, until you truly grasp the concept of shorting, don't try it. If you don't understand the concept, it's like playing a game without knowing the rules or playing while wearing a blindfold, and that's a very risky game to play when your money's on the line.

TAKE TWO . . . AND THREE

What does shorting mean? I'll try to define it a couple more times but I think you'll understand it better when I explain *how* it works. After all, it's harder to define the game of football than to explain *how* it's played.

Take two. Shorting is the opposite of going long. That is, short sellers make money if the stock goes down in price; long investors make money if the stock goes up in price. Trading or investing long refers to investing money the old fashioned way—buying an asset, holding on to it while it hopefully appreciates in value, and selling it to make a profit. An investor in a short transaction only makes money if the stock falls in value.

In terms of supply and demand, the person going short expects more sellers than buyers to drive the stock's price down; the person going long expects more buyers than sellers to drive the stock's price up.

Take three. A short sale occurs when an investor—usually a short-term trader—sells borrowed stock from a broker with the expectation that the stock's price will fall. Those shares are then sold on the market and the proceeds from the sale are credited to your brokerage account. These proceeds comprise the "loan" so, at this point, you have no access to them.

At some point, you must buy the shares back. If your expectation proves correct and the stock's price falls, you then buy the shares back at a lower price ("covering the short"). The borrowed stock then is returned to the broker and you keep the profits (less the commissions and any interest owned on the loan).

Regardless of whether the stock's price goes down or up, people who short a stock have committed themselves to buy the stock back to close their short position with the lender (the broker). The risk in doing this is that, if the stock goes up instead of down, you must buy it back at the higher price and take the loss. You then pay "margin interest" for the loan of the stock that your broker let you borrow from the proceeds that you received when you shorted the stock.

HOW DOES SHORTING WORK, ALREADY?

Okay, enough definitions. Let's explore *how* an investor makes (or loses) money when shorting.

A short transaction only has two steps:

1. Choosing a stock to short (entering the trade)
2. Closing the short (exiting the trade)

You do nothing else between those two steps except keep track of your shorting choices. (See, it seems easier already.) Why would you initiate a transaction to short a stock? Because you have reason to believe that the stock is on the verge of dropping in price.

A Fictional Example

A company called Toilets for Dogs (TFD) has been successful for a while, but you have reason to believe that the price is going to drop from its current cost of $70 per share. You based this theory on the fact that TFD was a successful novelty for awhile but now you have objective reasons to believe that the cost of the stock will drop now or very soon. You decide to short 100 shares at the current market price of $70 per share.

Your broker lends you 100 shares of TFD at $70 per share for a total of $7,000. In essence, you have borrowed those stocks. Those shares are then sold on the open market to another individual investor or institution and the proceeds ($7,000) are credited to your brokerage account for the time being.

One of two things can happen after you enter the short trade and before you are ready to close the short (exiting the trade and returning the borrowed shares to your broker):

1. The stock's price can drop as you anticipated.
2. The stock's price can rise to your chagrin.

If the price of TFD drops as you anticipated, let's say to $25, you can buy the stock back at the lower price ($25) and make a profit on the difference between the purchase price ($70) and the sales price ($25). Your borrowed shares then are returned to the broker

TFD Sinks in Price from $70 to $25

Borrowed and sold 100 shares of TFD @ $70	$7,000
Bought back and returned 100 shares of TFD @ $25	$2,500
Your Total Short Profits	+$4,500
	($7,000 − $2,500)

You made a nice profit of $4,500 because your cumulative shares dropped in value by that amount. The broker/lender sends you the difference or puts it into your account, depending on your arrangement.

However, if the price of TFD rises let's say to $100, you have to buy it back at the higher price—adding your own money to meet the difference. In this transaction, you lose money. The borrowed shares then are returned to the broker.

TFD Rises in Price from $70 to $100

Borrowed and sold 100 shares of TFD @ $70	$7,000
Bought back and returned 100 shares of TFD @ $100	$10,000
Your Total Short Losses	− $3,000
	($7,000 − $10,000)

You lost $3,000 because your cumulative shares *rose* in value by that amount and now you have to pay the difference to your broker/lender out of your own pocket. This is the danger of shorting: You *have to* buy back the shares you initially borrowed and sold. Whether the price is higher or lower when you decided to end the shorting transaction, you must buy back the shares at some point.

In either case, whether the stock goes up or down, the interest charged by your broker that accrued during the duration of your loan is deducted from your account. Your profit or loss is also diminished by the commission expenses.

A True Example

The example in Figure 10.1 is a real stock (QLogic Corporation) that showed three shorting opportunities in less than a month. The pricing boxes with red arrows (signaling when to short) and green arrows (when to get out of the short by buying the stock back) have been superimposed on the Wize-trade™ chart to demonstrate the visual factors that you should look for to signal a good short-trading opportunity and the exit points at which to get out of a short trade. (Note that the red lines appear here as black, and the green lines as gray.)

In reference to Figure 10.1, the following table shows the date and price of the three short-trading opportunities, the exit dates, the price of the stock at the time it was best to buy it back (the point at which there's an indication that the stock price is going back up), and the profits that could have been taken by shorting during these three periods.

Date of short signal	Stock price	Date of buy-back signal	Stock price at buy-back	Potential profit per share while shorting
6/19/02	45.72	6/26/02	35.00	+10.72 (45.72 – 35.00)
6/28/02	39.16	7/2/02	34.91	+4.25 (39.16 – 34.91)
7/8/02	39.68	7/11/02	36.67	+3.01 (39.68 – 36.67)
				Potential total short profits per share: $17.98

The potential per-share profit on these trades is $17.98—a 39 percent profit in less than a month (based on the original $45.72 price and the $17.98 profit). This potential 39 percent profit was made even though the actual value of the stock during this trading cycle *lowered* from $45.72 to $36.67.

FIGURE 10.1 *Example of a Good Short Trade*

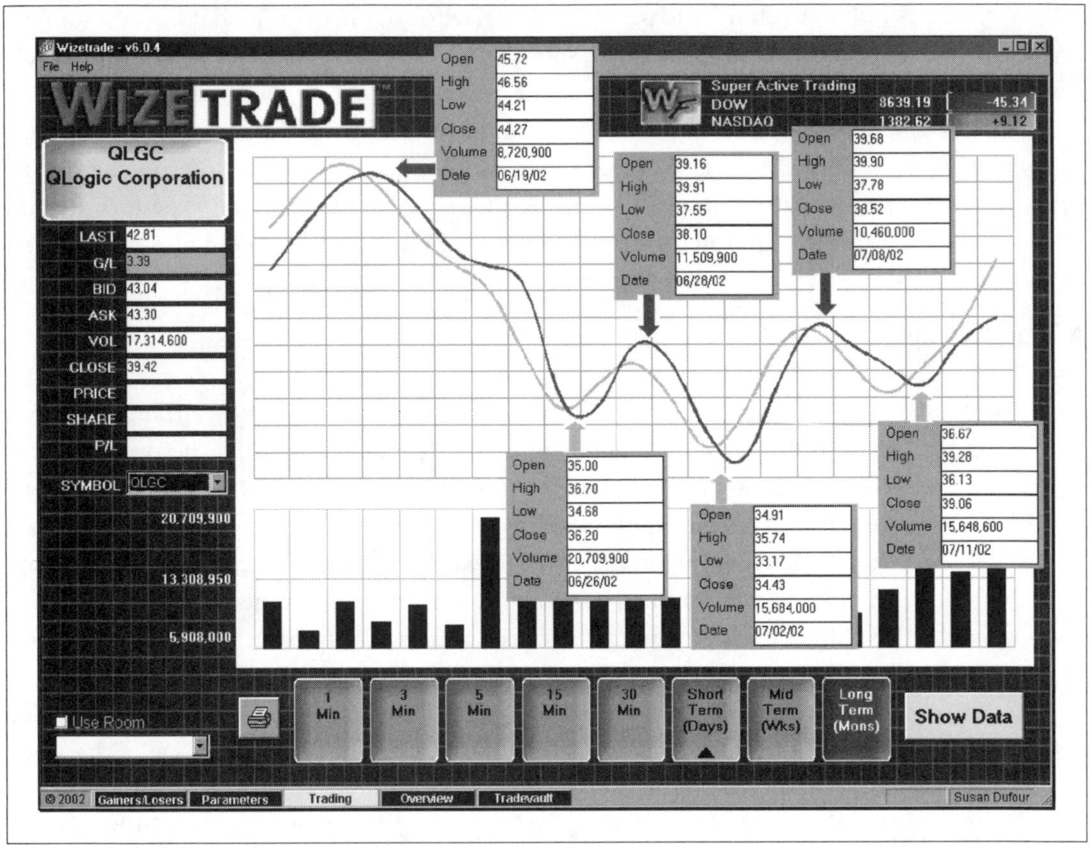

If the investor had 100 shares at $17.98 profit per share, the total profit in shorting this stock was $1,798. Again, this profit would have been made in less than a month on a stock that *lowered* in value by about $9 per share.

The investor could have potentially profited by 39 percent on short trading this stock just by paying attention to easily identifiable key indicators (fresh cross, strong angle, and good separation) and recognizing when to short this stock and when to buy it back three times in less than a month.

MAJOR CONSIDERATIONS FOR GOING SHORT

- Market direction
- High-priced stocks

- Catch the wave
- Volume
- Paper trading and radar screens

In order to recognize good shorting opportunities, you need a research tool (like Wizetrade™) or other resources to recognize the overall market direction and a particular stock's current performance in regard to price, an uptrend on the verge of going down ("catching the wave" based on buyer/seller pressure), and the volume being traded.

Market Direction

When looking for stocks to short, pay careful attention to the overall market direction. If the market is cycling down (money is flowing out of the market), there will often be more shorting opportunities. Instead of the overall market, you might concentrate on a particular sector—a group of securities in the same industry, like in healthcare or transportation. If a sector has an overall downtrend, then that sector may have several ripe shorting prospects.

If the market trend is going up, it is still possible to successfully short a particular stock but you need to be even more attentive because you're swimming against the tide by fighting the overall trend. When in doubt, don't fight market trends; go with the flow if you're not comfortable with shorting.

High-Priced Stocks

When shorting, look for high-priced stocks because you need room for the stock to fall; the bigger they are, the farther they can fall. Higher-priced stocks provide a greater opportunity for bigger profits when shorting. Obviously, an $80 stock has more room to fall than an $8 stock. If you short an $80 stock that drops 25 percent ($20) as opposed to an $8 stock that also drops 25 percent ($2), you would make $18 more profit by shorting the higher-priced stock.

Catch the Wave

The best opportunity to short a stock is when it's at the top of a long up-trend (the price has increased for awhile due to buying pressure) and you can recognize the moment it "runs out of gas" and starts heading down due to selling pressure. It is natural for *all* stocks to occasionally come down; no stock continually goes up.

If you catch a fresh cross when a stock *begins* to go down after enjoying a long uptrend, then you can maximize your profits by shorting at the highest price possible and completing the transaction at the end of the downward cycle just before it resumes heading up.

When stocks go up, they tend to chug up slowly; when they go down, they tend to plunge like they were falling off a cliff. The cycle is like a rollercoaster chugging slowly to reach the apex and then racing down to the bottom. These are natural up-and-down tendencies, so you can expect similar results during each cycle.

Volume

You want short orders to be processed fast—both when entering and exiting—to ensure that you will have no problem completing the transaction when you buy the stock back to cover the short. Therefore, volume is a very important factor when shorting. You want a stock that has a lot of activity (that is liquid) instead of one that's stagnant on the market.

For short trades, I recommend making sure that a stock has experienced a minimum trading volume of 600,000 shares daily on average, over the course of the past ten days or so. The higher the volume, the better your opportunity will be to get in and out of short trades when *you* want to rather than when the market makers dictate that you can. (See "Other Risks" later in this chapter.)

Paper Trading and Radar Screens

If you have never short traded before, I implore you to paper trade—practice, practice, practice—until you get the procedures and criteria that work for you down pat. "Pretend" that you make short trades and then carefully note the results (e.g., if you could have chosen a better entry point, what happened after the short was enacted, and if you could improve on pinpointing an exit point).

By putting trades on your radar screen (monitoring and looking for clear movement and signals until a good short opportunity arises), you can learn to successfully choose short trade opportunities without losing money. Like when paper trading, no harm, no foul.

SHORTING WITH BROKERS: MARGIN TRADES

In Chapter 4, I made a distinction between the two types of accounts you may have with a broker: a cash account, in which you provide money up front as a deposit, and a margin account, in which you borrow money from the broker to make transactions and pay interest on the loan. Both accounts are subject to fees or commissions per trade.

The way the rules are set up for shorting, there is no getting around short-trading with a margin account. You cannot conduct shorts with a cash account so you *must* set up a margin account to short. Make sure you read your broker's margin agreement and understand its implications. (As when applying for any loan or credit line, not everyone qualifies.)

When shorting, you are loaned the stock on margin by your broker. When someone buys your stock, your broker holds on to that money in your account as collateral to make sure you cover the short. If your stock goes in the red (if the share price rises), you pay interest on what you're losing until you cover the short transaction by buying back the stock.

For example, if you short 100 shares of a stock costing $50 each, the broker holds onto the $5,000 in your margin account. Hopefully, the share's price will drop lower so you can make a profit. However, if the share price increases to $60, then you not only owe $1,000 ($10 times 100 shares) but you also pay interest on that amount until you cover (buy back) the stock.

There's no limit to how high the price of a stock might rise—it can double (go up 100 percent), triple (up 200 percent), or go through the roof (the sky's the limit), and you must pay interest on your short as it goes up. Therefore, you should set an *absolute maximum loss* that you're willing to sustain before bailing out by covering the short. Stick to it. In contrast, when you go short on a stock using a margin account, the best it can do is to go down to zero, so the maximum gain is 100 percent.

OTHER RISKS

I've already mentioned that the risk of losses is unlimited because a stock's price has no ceiling when going up. Now let's cover some other risks to be aware of when shorting.

Short Interest and Short Squeeze

Short interest is the number of shares or percentage of a stock that has been sold short but has not yet been covered. Most stock exchanges track short interest in each stock and issue reports at the end of the month. This allows investors to see what short sellers are doing.

Rising short interest means that a growing number of people believe a stock will go down. High short interest indicates there will eventually be significant upward pressure on price when all the short sellers cover their short positions at the same time. You can see why it is advisable not to short a stock with high short interest.

If a stock starts to rise and a large number of short sellers try to cover their positions at the same time, it can quickly drive up the price even further. Your incentive is to cover before your fellow shorters do—to beat them to the punch—because as the buying pressure increases with all the short traders covering their positions, the price increases, which is the opposite of what you want.

Many times in a down market, you will see a stock spike up in volume and price. This is often due to individual and institutional traders filling their short positions. This volatility is the reason you want to have high volume/liquidity in a stock that you short. You need to be able to cover your position when the supply is high, not when it's limited because you'll have trouble finding a buyer.

Short and Distort

"Short and distort" takes place when traders manipulate stock prices in a bear market by taking short positions and then use a smear campaign to drive down the target stocks even further. Unethical traders spread false information in an attempt to drive the price of a stock down and make a profit for themselves by selling short.

Short and distort is the reverse of "pump and dump" in which crooks buy stock in a long position and issue false information that causes the target stocks price to increase.

ETHICS

Shorting is legal and regulated. Yet there are traders who feel guilty about "betting against the home team" by shorting because they hope to make a profit on a stock going down. Others perceive short selling as unethical and bad for the market. However, shorting contributes to the market by providing liquidity, efficiency, and acting as a voice of reason in bull markets. Also remember that every transaction requires a seller (you as a shorter) *and* a buyer. You can't trick anyone into buying a stock you're shorting; they're going to buy it anyway. Because shorting provides a ready supply of sellers, short selling helps to maintain a liquid and rational market for those posed to buy.

If you short a stock, you eventually have to buy it back; that's the way it works. If you and a lot of other people short the same stock, it may cause the stock price to fall in the short term. Eventually, however, you and every other person shorting have to buy the stock back. This activity alone drives prices higher.

Shorting stocks is a great way to make money if you know what you're doing and have resources to choose good candidates. You're not hurting anybody, you're not hurting the market, and you're still more of a player in the market by going short than those who have pulled their money out of the market entirely and are sitting on the sidelines.

If you make some wise choices, you can make money not only when the stocks you own go up in price but also when the stocks you shorted fall.

11

EVALUATING 35,000 STOCKS IN SECONDS

Joy! Rapture! I've got a brain!

SCARECROW, *The Wizard of Oz*

In this book, you have learned how to clearly evaluate any stock in the market and recognize good trading opportunities. Now, how do you *find* those great stocks? Where the heck are they?

You can spend several hours a day on your own researching companies and stock markets while you dig for sound opportunities, but by performing your own hunt for a "perfect" trade candidate, you undoubtedly will miss some opportunities while you're looking—especially short-term trades due to their small windows of opportunity.

Another option is to explore software programs and online resources that can search far quicker than you can because they are computerized. Plus, you can program them to search for exactly what you're seeking. The more specific you are about your criteria, the better the program can perform.

How would you like to use a program that searches—in seconds—35,000 stocks in major stock markets to locate and identify potential trading candidates that meet your personal trading style and strategy? What if that program *also* took into account your parameters for a wise trade: the price per share that fits your budget and strategy, the minimum volume of activity you want, and your criteria for exploring long or short candidates—and scanned a variety of stock exchanges?

A software program called Wizefinder™ foots this bill. It was designed to be used in conjunction with Wizetrade™ and quickly scans major stock markets—representing 35,000 stocks—to find potential trading candidates that meet your trading style as well as the Wizetrade™ criteria. You can also narrow your search to meet the parameters you specify; I explain these parameter options in this chapter.

For illustrative purposes in this chapter, I utilize graphics from Wizefinder™. You do *not* need to subscribe to Wizefinder™ to find great candidates, but it's a pretty terrific tool, if I do say so myself.

I want to emphasize that I wrote this chapter so that it is valuable to *all* readers, whether they have Wizefinder™ or not.

BASIC PARAMETERS

Your trading budget and risk tolerance will define what type of trader you are. Choose parameters that meet your trading style and strategy. Figure 11.1 and the sections that follow take a look at parameters for price per share and volume activity on Wizefinder™'s basic parameter screen. Next, we'll choose whether to look at long or short candidates that meet these parameters.

Price per Share

You should set parameters for stock prices within a certain range that fits your budget and trading strategy. Wizefinder™ lets you pick any range of stock prices per share that you're interested in exploring. (In the basic parameters screen in Figure 11.1, we chose to search for stocks ranging from $10 to $40.) Obviously, the broader the price range, the more candidates you'll find.

Just remember that a $20 stock may be a great buy while a $50 stock may prove to be a stinker; it depends on the individual stock. That's why we designate other parameters and criteria.

Whatever price-per-share range you choose, make sure it fits your budget and your trading strategy.

FIGURE 11.1 *Example of the Wizefinder™ Basic Parameter Screen*

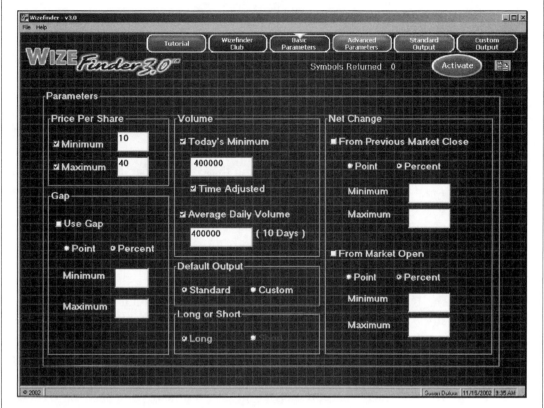

Volume

As I have often stressed before, it is very important to bear in mind trading volume when inspecting a stock. For example, you wouldn't want to get "stuck" in a stock of which you've got a large of number of shares that you can't sell because the stock isn't trading enough volume and therefore lacks liquidity. Lower volume could also mean a greater spread between the bid and ask which puts more money into the market makers' hands, not yours.

By default, Wizefinder™ sets a minimum trading volume of 300,000 shares per day. You'd like that to be the minimum *average* over the course of several days because consistency in volume is important. I would suggest that, depending on the situation, you look for the following minimum average volume:

- If you're going long, use an average daily volume of 400,000 over the course of ten days.
- If you're going short, it's a good idea to use an average daily volume of 600,000 over the course of ten days. This will reflect better liquidity which is what you want so that when you are ready to cover your short there will be a nice volume of shares traded and the price will reflect that good liquidity.

In the parameter screen in Figure 11.1, we chose 400,000 for Today's Minimum volume, we checked Time Adjusted, and chose 400,000 for Average Daily Volume (10 days). Let's look at these volume parameters one at a time.

Today's Minimum volume will limit the number of stocks returned to those that have traded a specified minimum number of shares at the current moment for that day. However, by using Today's Minimum without selecting Average Daily Volume, the list of potential trading candidates will include stocks that may be considered one-day wonders (those that spike up in volume for one day only) which are more volatile.

By using Today's Minimum and *Time Adjusted,* you'll limit the number of stocks returned to those that are on schedule to trade the minimum amount for the remainder of the trading day. For example, if it's 10:00 AM and you select a minimum amount of 400,000 along with Time Adjusted, the stocks returned may not have traded 400,000 shares *so far* that day, but if the volume continues at the current rate, it is projected that they will have traded at least 400,000 shares for the day.

By using *Average Daily Volume* (over the course of ten days), you will limit the number of stocks returned to those that have traded, on average, the number of shares you select over the past ten days. For example, if you select 400,000 as the Average Daily Volume (10 Days), the stocks returned will have traded on average 400,000 shares or more each day for the past ten days.

Also, by indicating an Average Daily Volume of hundreds of thousands of shares, you will avoid one-day wonders which may normally be selling relatively few shares, for example, 50,000 shares a day, but pop up to hundreds of thousands of shares one day due to a very unusual amount of buying or selling—no doubt due to institutional manipulation of the market. (If you are looking for one-day wonders—hopefully for relatively short-term trades that you keep a very close watch on—you can choose to view these candidates by clicking on One Day Wonders on the Advanced Parameters page.)

Long or Short

If the general direction of the market is going up, you'll find more trading opportunities by selecting the long option. Conversely, if the general direction of the market is going down, you'll find more trading opportunities by selecting Short. You can always take a look at both positions—Long and Short—to find as many good trading candidates as possible. In our example, we checked Long.

Other Basic Parameters

Though the layout of the output screen can be customized, we will look at the standard layout for our purposes. (Only Wizefinder™ users should be concerned with customizing. The same can be said for the Gap and Net Change parameters, which generally are not chosen by many users because they further narrow the trading candidates.)

ADVANCED PARAMETERS

Now let's switch screens to choose more parameters to help identify stocks that meet your specific trading strategy, namely your trading techniques and which stock exchanges to explore. Figure 11.2 shows this advanced parameter screen.

Trading Techniques

Wizefinder™ searches the markets for stocks that meet the traditional Wizetrade™ criteria and/or a combination of the following trading techniques (listed under Symbols Satisfying):

- *3 FAST Wizemen™*. This parameter finds stocks where the short-term (day), mid-term (week) and long-term (month) indicators are in agreement.
- *One-Day Wonders*. This parameter finds stocks where the short-term (day) indicator meets the Wizetrade™ criteria. The mid-term and long-term indicators are not considered.

FIGURE 11.2 *Example of the Wizetrade™ Advanced Parameter Screen*

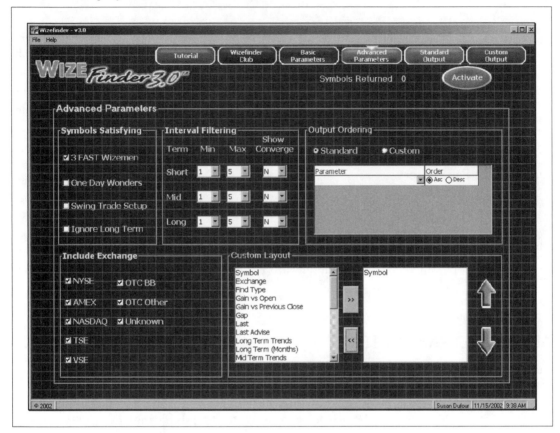

- *Swing Trade Setup.* This parameter finds stocks where the mid-term and long-term indicators are in agreement and the short-term indicator is the opposite color of the mid-term and long-term indicators and is *close* to making a cross or bounce. (This is useful for swing traders to find stocks to put on their radar screen to watch for when the short-term/day indicator *does* cross or bounce.)
- *Ignore Long-Term.* This parameter finds stocks where the short-term and mid-term indicators are in agreement. The long-term indicator is not considered.

In the example in Figure 11.2, we chose 3 FAST Wizemen™.

Stock Exchanges

Users may also filter their selection based on all the stocks in specific exchanges, including:

- New York Stock Exchange (NYSE)
- American Stock Exchange (AMEX)
- Nasdaq
- Two Canadian stock exchanges: TSE (Toronto) and VSE (Vancouver)
- Over-the-counter bulletin board (OTC BB)
- Over-the-counter other (OTC Other)
- Unknown exchanges

If all of these exchanges are chosen for scanning, Wizefinder™ searches for candidates among the 35,000 stocks represented by these exchanges and, within seconds, returns the results that meet the parameters you've chosen.

In our example, we chose all of the stock exchanges available.

Output Ordering

Under Output Ordering, you can choose the results to be presented in the standard format or you can customize the output to view whatever data you desire (choices are listed under Custom Layout) and in the order you want it displayed. This benefit allows the user to have the list sorted according to his or her particular trading concerns. However, for our purposes, we've chosen the standard format.

Activate for the Outcome Screen

At the top right-hand corner of any screen, you can click the Activate button to show a list of stocks that meet the selected parameters that you've chosen. You will be taken to either the standard or custom output screen that lists the stocks that meet your parameters and displays all the pertinent data plus several other informative categories.

Figure 11.3 displays on the standard output screen the symbols that are returned based on the sample parameters we selected for possible long trades.

FIGURE 11.3 *Exampleof the Wizefinder™ Output Screen for Long*

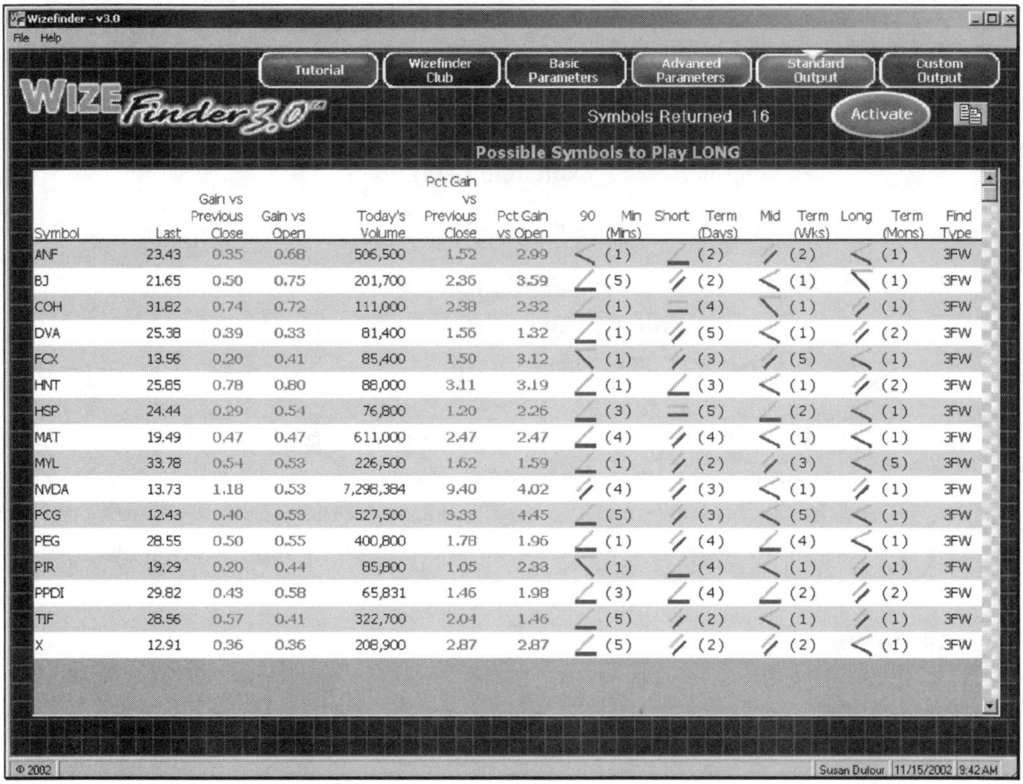

Symbol	Last	Gain vs Previous Close	Gain vs Open	Today's Volume	Pct Gain vs Previous Close	Pct Gain vs Open	90 Min (Mins)	Short Term (Days)	Mid Term (Wks)	Long Term (Mons)	Find Type
ANF	23.43	0.35	0.68	506,500	1.52	2.99	(1)	(2)	(2)	(1)	3FW
BJ	21.65	0.50	0.75	201,700	2.36	3.59	(5)	(2)	(1)	(1)	3FW
COH	31.82	0.74	0.72	111,000	2.38	2.32	(1)	(4)	(1)	(1)	3FW
DVA	25.38	0.39	0.33	81,400	1.56	1.32	(1)	(5)	(1)	(2)	3FW
FCX	13.56	0.20	0.41	85,400	1.50	3.12	(1)	(3)	(5)	(1)	3FW
HNT	25.85	0.78	0.80	88,000	3.11	3.19	(1)	(3)	(1)	(2)	3FW
HSP	24.44	0.29	0.54	76,800	1.20	2.26	(3)	(5)	(2)	(1)	3FW
MAT	19.49	0.47	0.47	611,000	2.47	2.47	(4)	(4)	(1)	(1)	3FW
MYL	33.78	0.54	0.53	226,500	1.62	1.59	(1)	(2)	(3)	(5)	3FW
NVDA	13.73	1.18	0.53	7,298,384	9.40	4.02	(4)	(3)	(1)	(1)	3FW
PCG	12.43	0.40	0.53	527,500	3.33	4.45	(5)	(3)	(5)	(1)	3FW
PEG	28.55	0.50	0.55	400,800	1.78	1.96	(1)	(4)	(4)	(1)	3FW
PIR	19.29	0.20	0.44	85,800	1.05	2.33	(1)	(4)	(1)	(1)	3FW
PPDI	29.82	0.43	0.58	65,831	1.46	1.98	(3)	(4)	(2)	(2)	3FW
TIF	28.56	0.57	0.41	322,700	2.04	1.46	(5)	(2)	(1)	(1)	3FW
X	12.91	0.36	0.36	208,900	2.87	2.87	(5)	(2)	(2)	(1)	3FW

The number of symbols returned can be found toward the top right-hand side of the screen.

On the far left, you can see the list of all of the stock symbols returned for possible long trades that meet the parameters we chose. If you have tailored Wizefinder™ for your personal trading strategy, you will get a handful of excellent trading candidates.

Most of the category headings for the returned data should be familiar to you. Let's concentrate on the four columns toward the right with symbols known as pictographs consisting of green and red lines. (The indication of 3FW under the Find Type heading at the far right refers to the 3 FAST Wizemen™ criteria at which we chose to look. If we'd chosen One Day Wonders, it would say ODW instead.)

Pictographs

Under the headings 90 Min. (Mins), Short Term (Days), Mid Term (Wks), and Long Term (Mons) are pictographs followed by a number in parentheses. The pictographs show the *general* direction of the green (buying) and red (selling) lines in the Wizetrade™ software.

This is important: The pictographs show the *general* directions and may not reflect the actual graphs in Wizetrade™. The green and red lines are depicted in one of three directions: up, flat, or down. Therefore, there is a possibility of nine different pictographs instead of the vast variations found in Wizetrade™. Therefore, you should always verify each trading candidate in Wizetrade™.

The number in parentheses to the right of the pictograph shows the number of time intervals since a fresh cross or bounce first occurred. If the letter "c" appears with the number it means that the green and red lines are converging. Because we're looking for separation instead of convergence, the preference would be to *not* choose stocks with "c" indicators (except in the case of a swing trade setup) or to put those stocks on our radar screen for future consideration. (Convergence is when the end of the green and red lines on the chart are pointing toward each other and coming closer together. It is possible that the lines will soon cross each other or they may "bounce" away from each other; this is wait-and-see time.)

Going Long

In the output screen in Figure 11.3, we chose to look at potential stocks for going long. Therefore you will notice that green lines (indicating buying pressure) are all on top of the red lines (indicating selling pressure). The pictographs give us a quick way to evaluate the criteria, but you need to know your objectives to know what to look for. Are you looking for a long-term position trade, an intermediate trade, or a swing trade? The following lists describe the direction of the lines (as you'd see them on the face of a clock) which you should concentrate on for each of these strategies when going long.

Long-term position trade (sort list by its mid-term pictograph).

- Day: green line pointing to one o'clock, red line pointing to three o'clock

- Week: parallel lines (green over red) going up; or green one o'clock, red three o'clock signaling a fresh cross on the week or month
- Month: parallel lines (green over red) going up signaling fresh cross on the week or month

Intermediate trade (sort list by its mid-term pictograph).

- Day: green at one o'clock, red at three o'clock
- Week: green at one o'clock, red at three o'clock signaling a fresh cross on the week
- Month: parallel lines (green over red) going up

Swing trade (sort list by its short-term pictograph).

- Day: green at one o'clock, red at three o'clock signaling a fresh cross on the day
- Week: parallel lines (green over red) going up
- Month: parallel lines (green over red) going up

A pictograph represented by green at two o'clock and red at four o'clock (known as an "alligator mouth" because it looks like open jaws) is least desirable. There is more volatility in this scenario since the sellers (red line) aren't as active as you would like them to be. With this wide angle, something will have to give—either the buying pressure will give way to the selling pressure or vice versa. We don't know at this point in time. (You don't want to get caught going the wrong way on a one-way street.)

Going Short

Now let's look at the standard output screen if we had chosen to go short with the same parameters we chose before (see Figure 11.4). The number of possible symbols to play short can be found toward the upper right-hand corner of the screen.

In this case, we chose to look at stocks for going short. Therefore you will notice that red lines (indicating selling pressure) are all on top of the green lines (indicating buying pressure). The following lists describe the direction of the lines that you should concentrate on for each strategy when going short.

FIGURE 11.4 *Example of the Wizefinder™ Output Screen for Short*

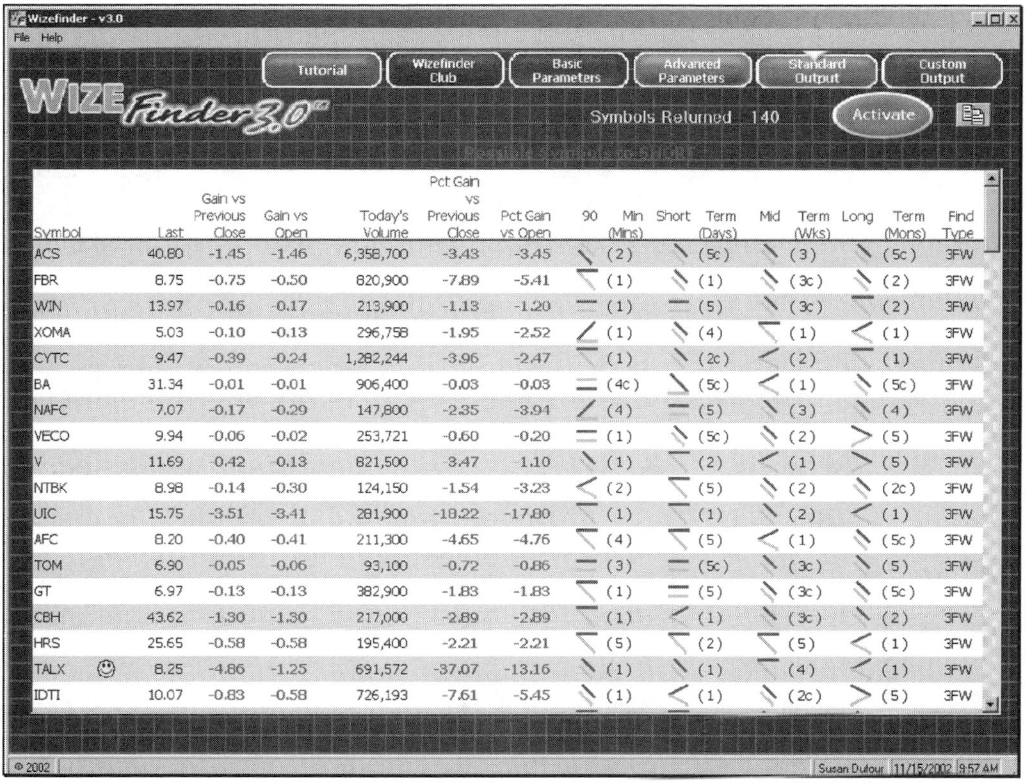

Symbol	Last	Gain vs Previous Close	Gain vs Open	Today's Volume	Pct Gain vs Previous Close	Pct Gain vs Open	90 Min (Mins)	Short Term (Days)	Mid Term (Wks)	Long Term (Mons)	Find Type
ACS	40.80	-1.45	-1.46	6,358,700	-3.43	-3.45	(2)	(5c)	(3)	(5c)	3FW
FBR	8.75	-0.75	-0.50	820,900	-7.89	-5.41	(1)	(1)	(3c)	(2)	3FW
WIN	13.97	-0.16	-0.17	213,900	-1.13	-1.20	(1)	(5)	(3c)	(2)	3FW
XOMA	5.03	-0.10	-0.13	296,758	-1.95	-2.52	(1)	(4)	(1)	(1)	3FW
CYTC	9.47	-0.39	-0.24	1,282,244	-3.96	-2.47	(1)	(2c)	(2)	(1)	3FW
BA	31.34	-0.01	-0.01	906,400	-0.03	-0.03	(4c)	(5c)	(1)	(5c)	3FW
NAFC	7.07	-0.17	-0.29	147,800	-2.35	-3.94	(4)	(5)	(3)	(4)	3FW
VECO	9.94	-0.06	-0.02	253,721	-0.60	-0.20	(1)	(5c)	(2)	(5)	3FW
V	11.69	-0.42	-0.13	821,500	-3.47	-1.10	(1)	(2)	(1)	(5)	3FW
NTBK	8.98	-0.14	-0.30	124,150	-1.54	-3.23	(2)	(5)	(2)	(2c)	3FW
UIC	15.75	-3.51	-3.41	281,900	-18.22	-17.80	(1)	(1)	(2)	(1)	3FW
AFC	8.20	-0.40	-0.41	211,300	-4.65	-4.76	(4)	(5)	(1)	(5c)	3FW
TOM	6.90	-0.05	-0.06	93,100	-0.72	-0.86	(3)	(5c)	(3c)	(5)	3FW
GT	6.97	-0.13	-0.13	382,900	-1.83	-1.83	(1)	(5)	(3c)	(5c)	3FW
CBH	43.62	-1.30	-1.30	217,000	-2.89	-2.89	(1)	(1)	(3c)	(2)	3FW
HRS	25.65	-0.58	-0.58	195,400	-2.21	-2.21	(5)	(2)	(5)	(1)	3FW
TALX ☺	8.25	-4.86	-1.25	691,572	-37.07	-13.16	(1)	(1)	(4)	(1)	3FW
IDTI	10.07	-0.83	-0.58	726,193	-7.61	-5.45	(1)	(1)	(2c)	(5)	3FW

Long-term position trade (sort list by its mid-term pictograph).

- Day: red at three o'clock, green at five o'clock
- Week: red at three o'clock, green at five o'clock; or parallel lines (red over green) going down signaling a fresh cross on the week or month
- Month: parallel lines (red over green) going down signaling a fresh cross on the week or month

Intermediate trade (sort list by its mid-term pictograph).

- Day: red at three o'clock, green at five o'clock

- Week: red at three o'clock, green at five o'clock signaling a fresh cross on the week
- Month: parallel lines (red over green) going down

Swing trade (sort list by its short-term pictograph).

- Day: red at three o'clock, green at five o'clock signaling a fresh cross on the day
- Week: red at three o'clock, green at five o'clock; or parallel lines (red over green) going down
- Month: parallel lines (red over green) going down

A pictograph represented by red at two o'clock and green at four o'clock (an "alligator mouth") is least desirable because there is more volatility in this scenario. The buyers aren't as active as you would like them to be. Just as when going long, either the selling pressure will give way to the buying pressure or vice versa. Again, we don't know at this point in time.

Going with the Flow

When we looked at both the long and short output screens, we saw the number of possible trading candidates that were found for each strategy. What if the number for the long or short candidates greatly outnumbered the candidates of the other? What should we glean from a big discrepancy between the number of long and short candidates?

Let me relate a true story that will help me explain.

When I first visited the campus of North Texas State where I went to school, I tried to get my bearings by driving around looking for buildings. I didn't think I knew any students or faculty there, however, the occupants of every car I passed going the other way waved at me. Being from Texas, I waved back, wondering if I knew them. Then cars started blowing horns and flashing lights at me. I thought, "These folks are awful friendly here." I must have looked like a fire truck as I flashed my lights and honked my horn in return. Finally, I noticed a one-way sign. I was going the wrong way.

Wizefinder™ tells you when you're going the wrong way. If you run a scan of the 35,000 stocks and find only 5 stocks on the long side and 120 stocks on the short side, yet you still are trying to go long, Wizefinder™ tells you that you're going the wrong way.

It also tells you when to go to cash and stay out of the market altogether. Cash is always a viable option as opposed to trading. If you run a scan for long trades and only a couple of stocks are returned, it's a warning to not go long. If you run a scan for short trades and only a couple come back, you would be well advised not to be trading short.

Going back to my flying story from Chapter 9, there are days when you wish that you were in the air while you're sitting on the ground but that's better than being in the air and wishing you were on the ground. Wizefinder™ is an invaluable tool that identifies the overall market condition and direction, whether it's intraday or over the course of days, weeks, or months.

If there is an overwhelming trend for longs or shorts, you can either go with the flow or take your chances in going the opposite direction—but at least you'll know what you're getting into.

EXCEL-LENT POSSIBILITY

Once your list of stocks is on the screen, you may export this information to a Microsoft Excel spreadsheet by clicking on the export icon in the upper right-hand corner of the screen (it looks like two overlapping pieces of paper). This allows you to save your list in an Excel file and make notations about the stocks you selected and why you decided to trade or not trade a particular stock. This will be beneficial over time, especially if you add a notation in Excel about why you chose to trade a particular stock. You can learn from your successes and your mistakes.

TALKING TO WIZETRADE™

A big time saver is the ability to drag and drop Wizefinder™ opportunities into Wizetrade™ for further analysis. Wizefinder™'s purpose is to help you quickly find candidates. While it shows basic criteria, you need to see the in-depth charts found in Wizetrade™ so you can analize the stock more completely. After all, we only use nine pictographs in Wizefinder™ so it cannot be as specific or show the long-term trends as the charts in Wizetrade™.

Here are seven steps to success while utilizing Wizefinder™ and Wizetrade™:

In Wizefinder™:
1. Set your basic and advanced parameters
2. Select long or short
3. Activate Wizefinder™ to scan the stock exchanges
4. Transfer a resulting stock symbol into Wizetrade™

In Wizetrade™:

1. Verify charts for fresh cross or bounce
2. Verify charts for good angle and separation in the short term (days), mid-term (weeks) and long term (months)
3. Check *all* indicators for fresh crosses to time your entry

Happy trails and happy trading!

George Thompson and Marc Sparks

Greg Schardt and George Thompson

George Thompson, Zig Zigler, Marc Sparks

Mark McDonnell

Marc Sparks, George Thompson, Senator Bob Dole

Senator Bob Dole and George Thompson

George Thompson at GlobalTec Solutions Office

GlobalTec Solutions Team

Mark McDonnell, Ron Points, Jack Kyne, George Thompson

WizeFEST 2002

Las Vegas Money Show

WiseFEST 2002

Marc Sparks and George Thompson, Studio Production

HOW TO READ STOCK TABLES

Truth be told, most people are baffled by the stock tables and quotations bombarding them on TV and over the Internet. Perhaps the only people you ever see scouring the zillions of stock quotes in the financial pages of the newspaper are those you pass in First Class as you drag your carry-on back to coach (Who are they trying to impress?!) If you own a bird, those pages most likely are the first to line its cage.

I suspect that many folks are intimidated to ask how to decipher these quotes because they think "I should know that, but I don't want anyone to know I don't have a clue." Well, there's nothing to be embarrassed about. If you don't understand these quotes, you're in the majority. Believe me. I don't want to turn this into a conspiracy, but remember when I said that Wall Street institutions wanted us to be clueless so we'll blindly follow their advice and pay dearly for it. Why should stock tables be any different?

The truth shall set you free. Here's the scoop.

IN THE NEWSPAPER

You've probably noticed the long columns of numbers and symbols at the back of the financial section of your newspaper. Although they may seem con-

FIGURE A.1 *Sample Stock Table*

52 W HIGH	52 W LOW	STOCK	TICKER	DIV	YIELD %	P/E	VOL 00S	HIGH	LOW	CLOSE	NET CHG
s45.39	19.75	ResMed	RMD	0.00	0.00	52.5	3831	42.00	39.51	41.50	-1.90
11.63	3.55	Revlon A	REV				162	6.09	5.90	6.09	+0.12
77.25	55.13	RioTinlo	RTP	2.30	3.2		168	72.75	71.84	72.74	+0.03
31.31	16.63	RitchieBr	RBA			20.9	15	24.49	24.29	24.49	-0.01
8.44	1.75	RiteAid	RAD			31028	4.50	4.20	4.31	+0.21
s38.63	18.81	RobtHall	RHI		26.5	6517	27.15	26.50	26.50	+0.14
51.25	27.69	Rockwell	ROK	1.02	2.1	14.5	6412	49.99	47.00	47.54	+0.24
↑	↑	↑	↑	↑	↑	↑	↑	↑	↑	↑	↑
1	2	3	4	5	6	7	8	9	10	11	12

fusing at first, these columns—referred to as stock tables or listings—are the heart of the financial pages.

The stock tables list just about every publicly traded company in the United States and include a summary of its market activities from the previous day and other crucial information about the company and its stock. Securities listed include stocks (both common and preferred), bonds, money market funds, and mutual funds.

Once you adjust your eyes to the fine print, reading the stock tables is really quite simple. Figure A.1 is a sample stock table, and Figure A.2 provides descriptions of all the elements of this table.

In addition to these standard abbreviations, the stock tables in the *Wall Street Journal* (and other newspapers) often include other symbols indicating a variety of factors, such as stock splits, dividend changes, first day of trading, new 52-week high or low, warrants, and many other relevant conditions. The financial section provides a key to explain the symbols or abbreviations for these categories.

Another interesting note is that the prices you used to see that included ½, ¾, etc., have been changed to decimals. In 2001, the NYSE became the first U.S. market to adopt this practice of trading in dollars and cents instead of fractions.

READING A QUOTE ON THE INTERNET

Today, it's far more convenient and accessible for most folks to get stock quotes off the Internet. This method is superior to printed quotes because most Web sites:

FIGURE A.2 *The Elements of a Stock Table*

Column #	Column Heading	What It Means
1	52 W High	The highest prices paid for the stock during the past year.
2	52 W Low	The lowest prices paid for the stock during the past year.
3	Stock	The name of the company. If there are no special symbols or letters following the name, it is a common stock. Different symbols imply different classes of shares, for example, "pf" means the shares are preferred stock.
4	Ticker	This ticker symbol is the unique alphabetic name identifying the stock. If you don't know what a particular company's ticker is, you can search for it online at <www.finance.yahoo.com>.
5	Div	Short for dividend. A dividend is when a public company decides to pay a portion of its profits to stockholders. For each share of stock owned, a shareholder should receive the listed price from the company's annual profits.
6	Yield %	The yield, or rate of return, on a stockholder's investment. It is figured by dividing the annual dividend by the current price of the stock.
7	P/E	Short for price/earnings ratio. The price of a share of stock divided by the company's earnings per share for the last year.
8	Vol 00s (or Sales 00s)	The total amount of stock traded during the previous day with the last two digits dropped off (i.e., a listing of 3831 translates as 383,100).
9	High	The highest price paid for the stock during the previous day.
10	Low	The lowest price paid for the stock during the previous day.
11	Close (or Last)	The last/closing price paid for the stock at the end of the previous day. If the closing price Is up or down more than 5 percent than the previous day's close, the entire listing for that stock is boldfaced. Keep in mind, you are not guaranteed to get this price if you buy the stock the next day because the price is constantly changing, but it's an approximation of what you might expect to pay.
12	Net Chg (or Chg)	The difference between the last trade and the previous day's price.

- Update throughout the day (some more often than others)
- Give you more related information, news, charting, research, etc.

Also if you don't understand an abbreviation, you usually can click on it to find out what it means. (Because each site tailors its presentation to be unique, they're all a little different, however, they try to make this information as accessible as possible to new "visitors.")

To get quotes, simply enter the ticker symbol in the quote box of any major financial site.

FIGURE A.3 *Sample Online Stock Table*

How to Read a Quote on the Internet

MICROSOFT CP (NasdaqNM: MSFT)

Last Trade 4:00pm - 50.05	Change -2.07 (-3.97%)		Prev Cls 52.12	Open 52.53	Volume 32,202,000	MSFT 3-MAY-2002
Day's Range 49.996 - 52.676	Bid 50.06	Ask 50.09	P/E 43.43	Mkt Cap 271.0B	Avg Vol 29,219,272	
52-wk Range 47.50-76.15	Bid Size 1,000	Ask Size 1,000	P/S 10.19	Div/Shr N/A	Div Date 26-Mar-99	
1y Target Est 71.89	EPS (ttm) 1.20	EPS Est 1.82	PEG 2.00	Yield N/A	Ex-Div 29-Mar-99	

The example in Figure A.3 shows a quote for Microsoft (MSFT) from Yahoo! Finance. You interpret the data in the same way you do in the newspaper, though again, quotes will be presented differently on various Web sites.

READING A STOCK TICKER ON TV

If you've ever watched a financial program on TV (perhaps CNBC or CNNfn), you've no doubt noticed those numbers scrolling along the bottom of the TV screen. This is known as a stock ticker, a presentation conceived by Thomas Edison, though today ticker tape has been replaced by an electronic scroll. Figure A.4 shows an example of a TV ticker scroll, and Figure A.5 presents the corresponding explanations.

Many streaming tickers use colors to distinguish how the stock is faring that day. Most TV stations use the following color scheme:

- *Green.* The stock is trading higher than the most recent closing price.
- *Red.* The stock is trading lower than the most recent closing price.
- *Blue or white.* The stock is unchanged from the most recent closing price.

FIGURE A.4 *Sample TV Ticker*

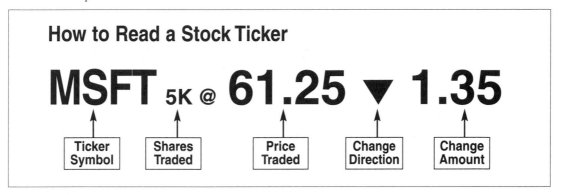

It's impossible for TV stations to report every single trade on their ticker tape because there are millions of trades made on over 10,000 different stocks every day. The TV station selects which trades to show based on factors such as volume, trading activity, price change, and how widely held a stock is.

FIGURE A.5 *The Elements of a TV Ticker*

Ticker Symbol	The unique characters used to identify the company; in this case Microsoft (MSFT).
Shares Traded	Volume of the trade being quoted. Abbreviations are K = 1000, M = 1,000,000, and B = 1,000,000.
Price Traded	Price per share for the particular trade
Change Direction	Shows whether the trade was higher or lower compared to the previous day's closing price.
Change Amount	The difference in price from the previous day's close.

agent A person who buys or sells for the account and risk of another. Generally, an agent takes no financial risk and charges a commission for his or her services.

arbitrage A technique used by alert traders, now aided by sophisticated computer programs, to profit from minute price differences for the same security on different markets. For example, if a computer monitoring markets notices that ABC stock can be bought on a New York exchange for $10 a share and sold on a London exchange at $10.12, the arbitrageur or a special program can simultaneously purchase ABC stock in New York while selling the same amount it in London, thus pocketing the difference.

averages A statistical tool for measuring the performance of securities markets. The most common is an average such as the Dow Jones Industrial Average, in which the prices of 30 industrial stocks are totaled and divided by a divisor that is intended to compensate for past stock splits and dividends. As a result, point changes in the average have only the vaguest relationship to dollar price changes in stocks included in the average.

bear market A term to describe a market of declining prices.

beta Coefficient measuring a stock's relative *volatility*. The beta is a covariance of the stock in relation to the rest of the stock market. The Standard & Poor's 500 Stock Index has a beta coefficient of 1. Any stock with a higher beta is more volatile than the market, and any with a lower beta can be expected to rise and fall more slowly than the market. A conservative investor whose main concern is preservation of capital should focus on stocks with low betas, whereas one willing to take high risks in an effort to earn high rewards should look for high-beta stocks.

bid and ask Collectively called the "quote," the bid refers to the highest price a buyer is willing to pay for a stock, while the ask is the lowest price a seller will accept.

broker An agent who acts as an intermediary between buyer and seller in trading securities, commodities, or other property. He charges a commission for this service.

capital gain Profit earned on the sale of securities, either through dividends or by selling the securities at a higher price than they originally cost.

capital stock All shares representing ownership of a business, including common and preferred.

capitalization Total amount of various securities issued by a corporation. Capitalization may include bonds, debentures, preferred and common stock, and surplus.

cash sale A transaction on the floor of a stock exchange that calls for delivery of the securities the same day. In regular stock trades, the seller is to deliver on the third business day. Bonds must be delivered on the next day after a trade.

collateral Securities or other property pledged by a borrower to secure repayment of a loan.

commission The broker's basic fee for purchasing or selling securities as an agent.

commission broker An agent who executes the public's orders for the purchase or sale of securities or commodities.

common stock Securities that represent an ownership interest in a corporation. If the company has also issued preferred stock, both common and preferred have ownership rights. Common stockholders assume the greater risk, but generally exercise the greater control and may gain the greater award in the form of dividends and capital appreciation. The terms *common stock* and *capital stock* are often used interchangeably when the company has no preferred stock.

competitive trader A member of an exchange who trades in stocks on the floor for an account in which there is an interest. Also known as a *registered trader.*

cumulative voting A method of voting for corporate directors that enables the shareholders to multiply the number of their shares by the number of directorships being voted on and to cast the total for one director or a selected group of directors. A 10-shareholder normally casts 10 votes for each of, say, 12 nominees to the board of directors. One thus has 120 votes. Under the cumulative voting principle, one may do that or may cast 120 (10×12) votes for only one nominee, 60 for two, 40 for three, or any other distribution one chooses. Cumulative voting is required under the corporate laws of some states and is permitted in most others.

day order An order to buy or sell which, if not executed, expires at the end of the trading day on which it was entered.

dealer An individual or firm in the securities industry who buys and sells stocks and bonds as a principal rather than as an agent. The dealer's profit or loss is the difference between the price paid and the price received for the same security. The dealer's confirmation must disclose to the customer that the principal has been acted upon. The same individual or firm may function, at different times, either as broker or dealer.

debit balance In a customer's margin account, that portion of the purchase price of stock, bonds, or commodities that is covered by credit extended by the broker to the margin customer.

delayed opening The postponement of the trading of an issue on a stock exchange because of unusual market conditions. Reasons for the delay might be an influx of either buy or sell orders, an imbalance of buyers and sellers, or pending corporate news that requires time for dissemination.

Depository Trust Company (DTC) The Depository Trust Company (DTC) is the world's largest securities depositary with more than $10 trillion worth of securities in custody. In 1995, DTC processed $41 trillion of securities through its book-entry settlement system. DTC is a national clearing house for the settlement of trade in corporate and municipal securities and performs securities custody-related services for its participating banks and broker-dealers. DTC is owned by members of the financial industry and by their representatives who are its users. DTC is 35.1 percent owned by the New York Stock Exchange on behalf of the Exchange's members. It is operated by a separate management and has an independent board of directors. It is a limited purpose trust company and is a member of the Federal Reserve.

director Person elected by shareholders, usually during an annual meeting, to serve on the board of directors of a corporation. The directors appoint the president, vice president, and all other operating officers. Directors decide, among other matters, if and when dividends shall be paid.

discretionary account An account in which the customer gives the broker or someone else discretion to buy and sell securities or commodities including selection, timing, amount, and price to be paid or received.

diversification Spreading investments among different types of securities and various companies in different fields.

dividend The payment designated by the board of directors to be distributed pro rata among the shares outstanding. For preferred shares, the dividend is usually a fixed amount. For common shares, the dividend varies with the fortunes of the company and the amount of cash on hand, and may be omitted if business is poor or if the directors determine to withhold earnings to invest in plants and equipment. Sometimes a company will pay a dividend out of past earnings even if it is not currently operating at a profit.

earnings report A statement issued by a company showing its revenues and expenses over a given period. The health of a company's earnings is what most investors consider when buying stock.

economic indicator A key statistic in the overall economy that experts use as a yardstick to predict the performance of the stock market.

equity Ownership in a company. Whereas bonds represent debt, stocks represent equity.

ex-dividend A synonym for "without dividend." The buyer of an ex-dividend stock is not entitled to the next dividend payment. Dividends are paid on a set date to all those shareholders recorded on the books of the company as of a previous date of record. For example, a dividend may be declared as payable to stockholders of record on a given Friday. Because three business days are allowed for delivery of stock in a regular transaction on the New York Stock Exchange, the exchange would declare the stock ex-dividend as of the opening of the market on the preceding Wednesday. That means anyone who bought it on or after that Wednesday would not be entitled to that dividend. When stocks go ex-dividend, the stock tables include the symbol "x" following the name.

fair market price A reasonable price for securities based on supply and demand.

free and open market A market in which supply and demand are freely expressed in terms of price. Contrasts with a controlled market in which supply, demand, and price may all be regulated.

fundamental research Analysis of industries and companies based on such factors as sales, assets, earnings, products or services, markets, and management. As applied to the economy, fundamental research includes consideration of gross national product, interest rates, unemployment, inventories, savings, etc.

good delivery Certain basic qualifications must be met before a security sold on an exchange may be delivered. The security must be in proper form to comply with the contract of sale and to transfer title to the purchaser.

good 'til cancelled (GTC) order An order to buy or sell that remains in effect until it is either executed or canceled. Also called an *open order*.

hypothecation The pledging of securities as collateral; for example, to secure the debit balance in a margin account.

Intermarket Trading System (ITS) An electronic communications network that links the exchanges of nine markets—New York (NYSE), American (AMEX),

Boston (BSE), Chicago (MSE), Cincinnati (CSE), Pacific (PSE), Philadelphia (PHLX), the Chicago Board Options Exchange (CBOE), and the NASD. The system enables market professionals to interact with their counterparts in other markets whenever the nationwide Consolidated Quote System (CQS) shows a better price. ITS was inaugurated on a pilot basis on April 17, 1978, with the New York and Philadelphia exchanges trading 11 stocks. During mid-1978, four other exchanges joined the system. Gradually, more issues were added. The Cincinnati Stock Exchange joined in February 1981. The NASD became a participant on May 17, 1982, when an experimental linkage between ITS and CAES, an automated system operated by the NASD, was ordered by the SEC. This pilot was originally limited to 30 listed stocks (23 on the NYSE and 7 on the AMEX) in which SEC Rule 19c-3 permits exchange member firms to make dealer markets in away from any exchange trading floor. The Chicago Board Options Exchange joined on February 20, 1991. The 3,293 issues eligible for trading on ITS at the end of 1994 represented most of the stocks traded on more than one exchange. Of these stocks, 2,817 are listed on the New York Stock Exchange and 476 on the American Stock Exchange.

investment bank Also known as underwriters, investment banks serve as middlemen between corporations issuing new securities and the buying public. Normally, one or more investment banks buy the new issue of securities from the issuing company for a negotiated price. The company walks away with this new supply of capital, while the investment banks form a syndicate and resell the issue to their customer base and the investing public. Investment banks perform a variety of other financial services, such as merger and acquisition advice and market analysis.

investment company A company or trust that uses its capital to invest in other companies. There are two principal types: the closed end and the open end, also known as a mutual fund. Shares of closed-end investment companies, most of which are listed on the NYSE, are readily transferable in the open market and are bought and sold like shares of stock. Capitalization of these companies remains the same unless action is taken to change, which is rare. Open-end funds sell their own new shares to investors, stand ready to buy back their old shares, and are not listed. Open-end funds are so called because their capitalization is not fixed; they issue more shares as people want them.

IRA (individual retirement account) An individual pension fund that anyone may open with a bank. An IRA permits investment of contributed funds through intermediaries like mutual funds, insurance companies, and banks, or directly in stocks and bonds through stockbrokers. Because it is intended for retirement, money in an IRA enjoys many tax advantages over traditional investments, but may not be withdrawn early without heavy penalty fees.

Keough plan Tax-advantaged personal retirement program that can be established by a self-employed individual.

limit order An order to buy or sell when and if a security reaches a specific price.

limit order processing The limit order system electronically files orders which are to be executed when and if the specific limit price is reached. The system accepts limit orders up to 99,999 shares and electronically updates the specialist's electronic book. Good 'til cancelled orders not executed on the day of submission are automatically stored until executed or cancelled.

liquidity (1) How easily one's assets can be converted back into cash. For example, money in an account that can't be withdrawn for ten years is not very liquid. (2) The ability of the market in a particular security to absorb a reasonable amount of buying or selling at reasonable price changes. Liquidity is one of the most important characteristics of a good market.

listed stock The stock of a company that is traded on a securities exchange. The various stock exchanges have different standards for listing. Some of the guides used by the New York Stock Exchange for an original listing are national interest in the company and a minimum of 1.1 million shares publicly held among not less than 2,000 round-lot stockholders. The publicly held common shares should have a minimum aggregate market value of $18 million. The company should have net income in the latest year of over $2.5 million before federal income tax and $2 million in each of the preceding two years.

long Signifies ownership of securities. "I am long 100 IBM" means the speaker owns 100 shares.

manipulation An illegal operation. Buying or selling a security for the purpose of creating false or misleading appearance of active trading or for the purpose of raising or depressing the price to induce purchase or sale by others.

margin The amount paid by the customer when using a broker's credit to buy or sell a security. Under Federal Reserve regulations, the initial margin required since 1934 has ranged from 40 percent of the purchase price up to 100 percent. Since 1974 the current rate of 50 percent has been in effect.

margin call A demand upon a customer to put up money or securities with the broker. The call is made when a purchase is made; also if a customer's equity in a margin account declines below a minimum standard set by the exchange or by the firm.

market-on-close (MOC) order A market order, which is to be executed in its entirety at the closing price, on an exchange, of the stock named in the order, and if not so executed, is to be treated as cancelled. The term *at the close order* shall also include a limit order that is entered for execution at the closing price, on an exchange, of the stock named in the order pursuant to such procedures as an exchange may from time to time establish.

market maker A broker/dealer who is registered to trade in a given security on the Nasdaq.

market order processing SuperDot's market order system is designed to process member firms' market orders of up to 30,099 shares. The system provides for rapid execution and reporting of market orders. In 1994, market orders were executed and reported back to the originating member firm on average within 24 seconds.

market order An order to buy or sell at the best price, currently available on the Trading Floor.

market price The last reported price at which the stock or bond sold, or the current quote.

market value The current resale value of a security. The market value of an issue is easily computed as the closing price multiplied by the shares outstanding.

member An individual that has trading privileges on the New York Stock Exchange. There are three ways to become a member:
1. *Purchase or lease a seat.* Currently, there is a fixed number of seats (1,366) on the NYSE. An individual must purchase or lease from someone who is already a member. The most recent seat sale was on March 1, 1999, for $2,600,000.
2. *Apply for physical access.* An individual pays an annual fee to the NYSE that allows access to the floor for trading.
3. *Apply for electronic access.* An individual pays an annual fee to the NYSE that allows all member privileges except the ability to trade on the floor.

member corporation A securities brokerage firm organized as a corporation, with at least one member of the New York Stock Exchange who is an officer or employee of the corporation.

member firm A securities brokerage firm organized as a corporation, partnership, or sole proprietorship with at least one member of the NYSE who is an officer or employee of the corporation.

NASD The National Association of Securities Dealers is an industry association of broker/dealers in the over-the-counter securities business. The NASD is self-regulatory body and administers the Nasdaq stock market.

Nasdaq An automatic information network that provides brokers and dealers with price quotations on securities traded over the counter; see *over-the-counter market*.

net change The change in the price of a security from the closing price of one day to the closing price on the next day on which the stock is traded. The net change is ordinarily the last figure in the newspaper stock price list. The mark +1 1/8 means up $1.125 a share from the last sale on the previous day the stock traded.

new issue A stock or bond sold by a corporation for the first time. Proceeds may be used to retire outstanding securities of the company, for new plants or equipment, for additional working capital, or to acquire a public ownership interest in the company for private owners.

New York Stock Exchange (NYSE) The NYSE marketplace blends public pricing with assigned dealer responsibilities. Aided by advanced technology, public orders meet and interact on the trading floor with a minimum of dealer interference. The result is competitive price discovery at the point of sale. Liquidity in the NYSE auction market system is provided by individual and institutional investors, member firms trading for their own accounts, and assigned specialists. The NYSE is linked with other markets trading listed securities through the Intermarket Trading System (ITS). NYSE-assigned dealers, known as specialists, are responsible for maintaining a fair and orderly market in the securities assigned to them. Most trading, however, is conducted by brokers acting on behalf of customers, rather than by dealers trading for their own account. For this reason, the NYSE is often described as an agency auction market. The interaction of natural buyers and sellers determines the price of a NYSE-listed stock.

odd lots Stock transactions that involve less than 100 shares.

offer The price at which a person is willing to sell a security.

options A derivative security that gives the holder the right to buy or sell a specified amount of the underlying security at a specific strike price and within a specified time frame. The purchaser hopes that the stock price will go up (if he or she buys a call) or down (if he or she buys a put) by an amount sufficiently above or below the strike price to provide a profit when the option is exercised. If the stock price holds steady or moves in the opposite direction, the price paid for the option is lost entirely. There are several other types of options available to the public but these are basically combinations of puts and calls. Individuals may write (sell) as well as purchase options. Options on stock indexes, futures, and debt instruments also exist.

over-the-counter (OTC) market A market for securities made up of dealers who may or may not be members of a securities exchange. OTC firms conduct business over the telephone and act either as principals or dealers (buying and selling stock from their own inventory and charging a markup) or as a broker or agent and charging a commission.

paper profit (loss) An unrealized profit (or loss) on a security still held. Paper profits (and losses) become realized only when the security is sold.

penny stocks Low-priced issues, often highly speculative, selling at less than $1 a share. Frequently used as a term of disparagement, although some penny stocks have developed into investment-caliber issues.

preferred stock A type of stock that pays a fixed dividend regardless of corporate earnings, and which has priority over common stock in the payment of dividends. However, it carries no voting rights, and should earnings rise significantly the preferred holder is stuck with the same fixed dividend while common holders collect more. The fixed income stream of preferred stock makes it similar in many ways to bonds.

price-earnings (PE) ratio A popular measure for comparing stocks selling at different prices in order to single out overvalued or undervalued issues. The PE ratio is simply the price per share divided by the company's earnings per share. However, PE is not always an accurate guide to a stock's quality. Some people tend to think that a stock is inflated and drastically overvalued if its price is many times its earnings. Yet that same stock may be quite accurately valued to reflect the company's rapid growth and potential for high future earnings. When comparing PEs it is therefore important to choose stocks in the same industry that are likely to face the same earnings prospects.

primary market The process by which a corporation's stock is issued for the first time. It is then sold to the public on the secondary market.

principal Any person who buys or sells a security for his or her own account. Also refers to an executive of a firm that actively engages in that firm's trading business.

program trade Program trading is defined as a wide range of portfolio trading strategies involving the purchase or sale of 15 or more stocks having a total market value of $1 million or more. One example is index arbitrage. Index arbitrage is defined as the purchase or sale of a basket of stocks in conjunction with the sale or purchase of a derivative product, such as index futures, in order to profit from the price difference between the basket and the derivative product. Other examples of program trading strategies are liquidation of facilitation's, liquidation of EFP stock positions, and portfolio management, which includes portfolio realignment and portfolio liquidations. The NYSE's program trading statistics are aimed at assessing the impact of these transactions on the normal functioning of the market. Daily program trading activity is calculated as the sum of shares bought, sold, and sold short in program trades. The total of these shares divided by total reported volume then provides a percentage which illustrates the relative importance of program trading during the period in question. This method is not the only way to measure program trading. One alternative would be to examine buy programs as a percentage of total purchases; another would be to examine sell programs as percentage of total sales. A third alternative is to calculate program purchases and sales as a percentage of total purchases and sales or twice total volume (TTV).

proxy A ballot by which stockholders can transmit their votes on corporate matters without needing to attend the actual shareholders meeting. A proxy could also state the stockholder's intention to transfer voting rights to someone else. A company's shareholders are commonly asked to vote on such matters as electing a board of directors, approving mergers and acquisitions, and sometimes on proposals that other stockholders have submitted to management. One share generally equals one vote.

quote The highest bid to buy and the lowest offer to sell any stock at a given time.

rally A brisk rise following a decline in the general price level of the market, or in an individual stock.

recession A period of no or negative economic growth and high unemployment.

registered competitive market maker Members of the New York Stock Exchange who trade on the floor for their own or their firm's account and who have an obligation, when called upon by an exchange official, to narrow a quote or improve the depth of an existing quote by their own bid or offer.

registered representative The person, normally employed by a brokerage firm or broker/dealer, who acts as an account executive for customers to buy and sell securities. The term *registered* means the individual has passed qualifying securities examinations and is registered with the SEC.

regular way delivery Unless otherwise specified, securities sold on the New York Stock Exchange are to be delivered to the buying broker by the selling broker and payment made to the selling broker by the buying broker on the third business day after the transaction. Regular delivery for bonds is the following business day.

Regulation T The federal regulation governing the amount of credit that may be advanced by brokers and dealers to customers for the purchase of securities.

Regulation U The federal regulation governing the amount of credit that may be advanced by a bank to its customers for the purchase of listed stock.

round lot order An order to buy or sell in multiples of 100 shares.

secondary distribution Also known as a secondary offering. The redistribution of a block of stocks some time after it has been sold by the issuing company. The sale is handled off of the exchange by one or more securities firms at a fixed price related to the market price. The block of stock is usually large, such as might be involved in the settlement of an estate.

secondary market When stocks or bonds are traded or resold, they are said to be sold on a secondary market. The majority of all securities transactions take place on a secondary market.

Securities and Exchange Commission (SEC) A watch-dog agency created by the U.S. Congress to monitor the securities industry and enforce punishments of those that violate the industry's regulations.

Securities Industry Association (SIA) Represents the collective business interests of more than 500 brokerages and investment banking firms. Membership includes most NYSE member organizations, major firms of all U.S. and Canadian exchanges, and the OTC market.

Securities Industry Automation Corporation (SIAC) The organization which operates the automation and communications systems of the New York Stock Exchange and American Stock Exchange to support trading, market data reporting, and surveillance activities. SIAC also supports the NSCC's nationwide clearance and settlement systems and it is the systems processor for industry-wide National Market System components, such as CTS, CQS, and ITS. SIAC is jointly owned by the NYSE and AMEX.

self-regulation The way in which the securities industry monitors itself to create a fair and orderly trading environment.

settlement The conclusion of a transaction in which parties pay for securities purchased and take delivery of securities sold.

short covering Buying stock to return stock previously borrowed to make delivery on a short sale.

short position Stock options or futures contracts sold short and not covered as of a particular date. On the NYSE, a tabulation is issued once a month listing all issues on the exchange in which there was a short position of 5,000 or more shares and issues in which the short position had changed by

2,000 or more shares in the preceding month. Short position also means the total amount of stock an individual has sold short and has not covered, as of a particular date.

short sale A transaction by a person who believes a security will decline and sells it, though the person does not own the security. For instance: You instruct your broker to sell 100 shares of XYZ. Your broker borrows the stock so delivery of the 100 shares can be made to the buyer. Your broker deposits the money value of the shares borrowed with the lender. Sooner or later you must cover your short sale by buying the same amount of stock you borrowed for return to the lender. If you are able to buy XYZ at a lower price than you sold it for, your profit is the difference between the two prices, not counting commission and taxes. But if you have to pay more for the stock than the price you received, that is the amount of your loss. Stock exchange and federal regulations govern and limit the conditions under which a short sale may be made on a national securities exchange. Sometimes people will sell short a stock they already own in order to protect a paper profit. This is known as selling short against the box.

specialist Central to the New York Stock Exchange customer-driven system is the specialist. Specialists manage the auction market in the specific securities allocated to them. Specialist units are independent companies in corporate or partnership structures. There are ten firms employing 482 specialists who specialize in more than 2,800 stocks. Specialists conduct trading in equities across a range of industries. The number of stocks traded by an individual specialist varies according to the total activity of the stocks. Specialist firms distribute the activity to balance the workload for each specialist. Most specialists manage between five and ten stocks. A specialist managing one of the most active issues would normally specialize in that stock and perhaps one less active stock. A specialist must maintain a fair, competitive, orderly and efficient market. This means that all customer orders have an equal opportunity to interact and receive the best price. It also means that once auction trading begins, a customer should be able to buy or sell a reasonable amount of stock close to the last sale. Therefore, a specialist works to avoid large or unreasonable price variations between consecutive sales. The results: almost 98 percent of all trades take place at 1/8 point or less from the last sale. The auction takes place at the specialist's post where the stocks are traded. This single location, or point of sale, combined with rules of trading, guarantees maximum order exposure, interaction, and market liquidity.

split The division of the outstanding shares of a corporation into either a larger or smaller number of shares, without any immediate impact in individual shareholder equity. For example, a three-for-one forward split by a company with one million shares outstanding results in three million shares outstanding. Each holder of 100 shares before the split would have 300 shares each worth less, although the proportionate equity in the company would stay the same. A reverse split would reduce the number of shares outstanding and each share would be worth more.

stock dividend A dividend paid in securities rather than cash. The dividend may be additional shares of the issuing company, or in shares of another company (usually a subsidiary) held by the company.

stop-limit order An order to buy or sell at a specified price or better, called a stop-limit price, but only after a given stop price has been reached or passed. It is a combination of a stop order and a limit order.

stop order An order to buy or sell at the market price once the security has traded at a specified price called the stop price. A stop order may be a day-limit order, a GTC order, or any other form of time-limit order. A stop order becomes a market order when the stop price is reached. A stop order to buy must always be executed when the buy price is at or above the stop price. A stop order to sell must always be executed when the sell price is at or below the stop price.

SuperDot (Super Designated Order Turnaround System) Transmits member firms' market and day limit orders, up to specified sizes in virtually all listed stocks, through the common message switch to the proper trading floor workstation. Specialists receiving orders through SuperDot execute them in the trading crowd at their posts as quickly as market interest and activity permit, and return reports to the originating firm's offices via the same electronic circuit that brought them to the floor. SuperDot can handle daily volume exceeding two billion shares.

syndicate A group of investment bankers who together underwrite and distribute a new issue of securities or a large block of an outstanding issue.

S&P 500 A capitalization-weighted index of 500 stocks. Standard and Poor's 500 index represents the price trend movements of the major common stock of U.S. public companies. It is used to measure the performance of the entire U.S. domestic stock market.

technical research Analysis of the market and stocks based on supply and demand. The technician studies price movements, volume, trends, and patterns which are revealed by charting these factors and attempts to assess the possible effects of current market action or future supply and demand for securities and individual issues.

tender offer A public offer to buy shares from existing stockholders of a company, usually made by another company attempting an acquisition. So-called because stockholders are asked to tender (surrender) their holdings for a premium above the current market price.

third market Securities listed on a stock exchange that are also traded in the over-the-counter market by broker/dealers.

tick The tick is the direction in which the price of a stock moved on its last sale. An up tick means the last trade was at a higher price than the one before it and a down tick means the last sale price was lower than the one before it. A zero-plus tick means the transaction was at the same price as the one before, but still higher than the nearest preceding different price. The tick becomes especially important when large market movements trigger the implementation of certain circuit breakers meant to stabilize the market.

treasury stock Shares, formerly outstanding, that were repurchased by the issuing company. Companies often repurchase stock to benefit existing shareholders. Those who sell receive a premium price from the company for their shares, thus substituting a large capital gain for future dividends. This ploy is used when dividend taxes are higher than capital gains taxes. Remaining investors who keep their shares benefit from a tightened supply, which raises the share price. Companies may later resell treasury stock or retire it according to a shareholder vote.

triple witching hour The last trading hour on the third Friday of March, June, September, and December when options and futures on stock indexes expire concurrently.

up tick A term used to designate a transaction made at a price higher than the preceding transaction. Also called a *plus tick*. A zero-plus tick is a transaction at the same price as the preceding trade but higher than the preceding different price. Conversely, a down tick or minus tick is a transaction made at a price lower than the preceding trade. A plus sign or minus sign is displayed throughout the day. They are attached to the last price of each stock and can be seen on the trading post at the floor of the New York Stock Exchange.

volatility A measure of the fluctuation in market price of a security. A volatile issue has frequent and large swings in price. Mathematically, volatility is calculated as the annualized standard deviation of returns.

volume The number of shares or contracts traded in a security or an entire market during a given period. Volume is normally considered on a daily basis, with a daily average being computed for longer periods.

voting right The common stockholders' right to vote their stock in the affairs of a company. Preferred stock usually has the right to vote when preferred dividends are in default for a specified period. The right to vote may be delegated by the stockholder to another person.

when issued A short form of *when, as, and if issued*. The term indicates a conditional transaction in a security authorized for issuance but not as yet actually issued. All when-issued transactions are on an "if" basis, to be settled if and when the actual security is issued and an exchange or NASD rules the transactions are to be settled.

George Thompson has revolutionized the method of analyzing stocks by creating an easy-to-use software program that the average investor can utilize to make intelligent trading decisions. His program, Wizetrade, is successfully used by thousands of traders across the globe each day. George's desire is to help level the playing field so that top Wall Street analysts are not the only ones that can increase their net worth. He feels that every person can benefit from the stock market given a little knowledge and the right tools.

Mr. Thompson hosts a nationally syndicated radio program, has appeared on television, and has educated thousands of people on the art of successful trading. His entrepreneurial leadership and dedication to taking the guesswork out of trading have been the cornerstone of his career.